D1131576

DATE DUE

12 - 19 - 62		
NOV 1 1965 NOV 9 1975		
NOV 0 6 1981		
GAYLORD		PRINTED IN U.S.A.

THE SAINT AUGUSTINE LECTURE SERIES

Saint Augustine and the Augustinian Tradition

PRESENTED UNDER THE AUSPICES OF

Villanova University

UNDER THE EDITORSHIP OF

Robert P. Russell, O.S.A.

THE MACMILLAN COMPANY
NEW YORK · CHICAGO
DALLAS · ATLANTA · SAN FRANCISCO
LONDON · MANILA

IN CANADA
BRETT-MACMILLAN LTD.
GALT, ONTARIO

THE SAINT AUGUSTINE LECTURE 1961

Charter of Christendom:
The Significance of
the *City of God*

JOHN O'MEARA

THE MACMILLAN COMPANY

NEW YORK 1961

Nihil obstat: Edward J. Montano, S.T.D.
Censor Librorum

2 8 0 .5
A u 4 5 c
O m 2

Imprimatur: ✠ Francis Cardinal Spellman
Archbishop of New York

July 26, 1961

The nihil obstat and imprimatur are official declarations that a book or pamphlet is free of doctrinal or moral error. No implication is contained therein that those who have granted the nihil obstat and imprimatur agree with the contents, opinions or statements expressed.

ACKNOWLEDGMENT

Saint Augustine, *The City of God*, Books I-VII translated by Demetrius B. Zema, S.J., and Gerald G. Walsh, S.J., with an introduction by Etienne Gilson (New York, Fathers of the Church, Inc., 1950); Books VIII-XVI translated by Gerald G. Walsh, S.J., and Grace Monohan, O.S.U. (New York, Fathers of the Church, Inc., 1952); Books XVII-XXII translated by Gerald G. Walsh, S.J., and Daniel J. Honan (New York, Fathers of the Church, Inc., 1954).

© Villanova University 1961

All rights reserved—no part of this book may be reproduced in any form without permission in writing from the publisher, except by a reviewer who wishes to quote brief passages in connection with a review written for inclusion in magazine or newspaper.

First Printing

The Macmillan Company, New York
Brett-Macmillan Ltd., Galt, Ontario

Printed in the United States of America

Library of Congress catalog card number: 61-15186

Introduction

The present work reproduces in a somewhat expanded form the third annual Saint Augustine Lecture delivered at Villanova University in the spring of 1961. Inaugurated in 1959, under the general theme of "Saint Augustine and the Augustinian Tradition," these yearly lectures are designed not only to promote a wider understanding and a fuller appreciation of the life, personality, and teachings of the great Doctor of the Church but also to stress the Saint's particular relevance and importance to the men and problems of our own age. And it is indeed a happy coincidence that the Saint Augustine Lecture should come into existence at a time that witnesses so great a renewal of interest in Saint Augustine and an ever increasing number of outstanding specialists in the field of Augustinian scholarship.

38227

Professor O'Meara's authority and eminence in Augustinian studies are widely recognized not only throughout the English-speaking world but also on the European continent. In selecting for his subject "The Significance of Saint Augustine's City of God," he reviews and evaluates for us the timeless and timely lessons of one of the richest documents in all Christian literature. Another Augustinian scholar has recently observed, "In no work of his is Augustine more fully presented than in the *City of God*."* Professor O'Meara's penetrating analysis of this masterpiece would appear to justify such a verdict.

The Saint Augustine Lecture Committee wishes to express its gratitude to Dr. Donald A. Gallagher, Vice Chairman of the Philosophy Department, for assistance in the final preparation of the manuscript for publication.

ROBERT P. RUSSELL, O.S.A.

Villanova University
Villanova, Pennsylvania

* Marthinus Versfeld, *A Guide to the City of God* (New York, Sheed & Ward, Inc., 1958), p. x.

Author's Preface

"As man amongst creatures, and the Church amongst men, and the Fathers in the Church, and St. Augustine amongst the Fathers, so amongst the many precious volumes, and in the rich store-house of his works, his books on the City of God have a special pre-eminence." So wrote W. Crashawe in a dedication to the Earls of Pembroke, Arundel, and Montgomery. So might one commend the *City of God* still as of all books, other than the Bible, the most significant and valuable for the understanding of Western Christendom.

Mr. Christopher Dawson in his recent *The Historic Reality of Christian Culture* (Religious Perspectives, Vol. I, 1960), in making a timely plea for the creation of chairs and courses in our universities in Christian Classics, writes: "The success of the old classical education was largely due to the fact that it limited itself to a single cultural tradition and was able to study it thoroughly. Nevertheless, as we have seen, the classical tradition was not the only unifying element in Western culture. The tradition of Christian culture is even more important and reaches far deeper into the European consciousness. For it is this and not science or humanism which was the spiritual bond that transcended the divisions and antagonisms of race and class and nationality and created that society of peoples which was the community of Western Christendom" (p. 109).

The following pages are intended to illustrate not only how important the *City of God* can be for an understanding of our past but also what comfort and help it can afford in these critical times and in face of an uncertain future.

Few are the books that have given rise to so much misconception as the *City of God*. By some it is thought to give a philosophy, by others a theology of history. By some it is thought to contain well-developed political theories, to be hostile to the State as such and in particular to the Roman Empire, and to outline the provinces of an Established Church and Christian State. By others it is understood to be so dominated by Platonic idealism that inevitably it led to a reaction against the institution of the Church and inspired thereby the Reformation. Again, it is considered to be primarily a Christian reply to the charge that Rome had been sacked because it had become Christian, as identifying the city of God with the

Mt. Mercy College Library,
Cedar Rapids, Iowa

Church, and as teaching that justice does not enter into the definition of the State.

More serious still: the teaching of Augustine on predestination, never accepted in its full rigor by the Church, is grim and somber in the *City of God*. The Pelagian controversy had tended to force him into some exaggeration, at least in his expressions, in relation both to Nature and to Grace. Yet when one has studied Augustine's life and works for long, one finds it difficult to believe that he was mainly a pessimist. One must expect, and indeed welcome, clear evidence of a countervailing optimism in keeping with so vital a person and one so unreservedly generous in the service of man.

The *City of God* is no more purely theoretical than it is purely theological. It is, of course, mainly theological; but it is also founded upon Augustine's own experience. It will be seen that it is an application of the theme of his own development and conversion, as described in the burning pages of the *Confessions*, to the broader, less immediate, canvas of man's destiny. Augustine's reflection upon his experience, especially at the time of his conversion, both in outline and in surprising precision in detail, is the key to much of his characteristic teaching.

We should take warning from this: however much he might regret some of the ingredients of his past, he was happy to recognize that through it and them Providence had brought him to where, humanly speaking, he felt more secure. His attitude, therefore, to these things could not be wholly negative and full of utter condemnation. On the contrary he formed from the pattern of his life a theory of providential economy that to many might seem both too living and too tolerant. If Rome and the philosophy of the Greeks could, for all their error, not only not prevent him from accepting Christ and the Christian Revelation, but actually lead him to do so, why should they not be as useful to others—to all mankind? It might seem paradoxical, for example, that the bitterest enemy of the Christians, Porphyry, should through his writing play a significant role (along with other Neoplatonists) in Augustine's conversion. This, however, was a fact, and Augustine was willing to take account of it in his notions of the dealings of Providence with men.

It can be said that although the scope of Augustine's writings is immense, they are animated by a few central ideas that came to him from the sensitive brooding on his own life. Thus the leading ideas of both the *Confessions* and the *City of God*, as we shall see very briefly, are anticipated in his first extant works. There we can see very clearly how close life and thought come in the mind of Augustine.

It is a commonplace to say that the age of Augustine was very like our own. We should remember that our view of his times is distorted by our looking at it from the vantage of over fifteen hundred years of Christian domination. Our view of our own times is too close to be in focus. We may not be able to see the present and the future as they are and will be; but at least we can make some attempt to strip the past of the encumbrances to our vision added later.

Some now speak of our living in post-Christian

times, and seem to imply that Christianity as a force in the world can but decline. When one contemplates the defection from Christianity and the scandal of its disunity on the one hand, and on the other the emergence upon the world's stage of the seething populations of non-Christian peoples—peoples who are as likely to assert their independence of Christianity as they are of Western political powers—one cannot feel a firm human confidence in the future of Western Christendom.

And yet, when Augustine was writing the *City of God*, his confident reading of the future cannot have seemed so justified to many of his contemporaries as it is to us now. The prospects of Christianity in the first quarter of the fifth century may have seemed bright; but we tend to forget that until that time the Church's history had been one, for the most part, of bare toleration and frequent persecution. Even within Augustine's own life there had been the pagan reaction under Julian the Apostate (361–363 A.D.). Even in the fifth century pagans had not lost all countenance. Again the decline of the powerful and closely integrated Empire of Rome, evident to all and admitted by Augustine, must have struck its citizens with a greater chill than that which affects in our day the loosely and vaguely associated West.

We should, then, note that the comparison of our situation to his is closer than, perhaps, is ordinarily realized. And we should take hope from his calm confidence at such a crisis in consciously drawing up in the *City of God* the charter for a Christian future, not only for Rome but for all the world.

The West is now tempted to despair. Should it not

rather trust that the very qualities that made it dominant in the past among the nations of the world will help it to survive the competition of great and ancient peoples now feeling their strength and anxious to body forth their cultures and traditions? The great lesson of the *City of God* is that out of all things comes good. Augustine saw clearly that in his time both Christianity and Rome would each benefit by the good that was in the other, and by any good from wherever else it might come. For Christianity assimilation meant acceptance that was universal in the context of his time. For Rome it meant a new birth and an even longer future. For Greek thought it meant transmission and development. The keynote of the *City of God* is fulfillment, not destruction.

In our time observers predict for the future either domination by one culture or a kind of democracy of cultures. Mr. Christopher Dawson writes: "Any claim on the part of the ancient world-cultures to possess a tradition of universal validity represents a kind of cultural imperialism which is no less unpopular than the military and economic imperialism of the Great Powers. In its extreme form [the] idea of 'cultural democracy' is obviously inacceptable. We cannot regard the culture of a particular Melanesian people or even the Melanesians as a whole as in any sense equivalent to the culture of China or India. Nevertheless the tendency to cultural relativism is just as strong among the scholars who have made a lifetime's study of the problems of civilization. We see a striking example of this in the case of Dr. Arnold Toynbee, whose whole work is based on the philosophical equivalence of cultures and who rejects the idea of the unity of civilization as a one-sided simplification of history due to the pride and provincialism of Western historians" (*op. cit.*, p. 102).

One must obviously follow Mr. Dawson in trying to work toward a middle way between the domination of one culture and a proletariat of cultures. Here it would be wrong of us to think that the culture of the Christian West should not suffer accidental change. One might ask oneself if the very first followers of Christ could have imagined the Christendom that was ushered in in Augustine's own period. Augustine's attitude to its future in turn was in no way static: he did not believe that the end of the world was at hand; he did not believe that Christianity could not profit, in a human way, from other things. Christianity was a leaven, an acorn. Who could say that it was not at work within the mass? Who could say that the tree was fully grown and that it had taken its final unalterable shape?

The practical problem with which Augustine had—and Christianity still has—to deal was the problem of the spiritual Church in a secular world: the city of God in the city of this world. It is of the first importance to understand that he did not condemn out of hand the city of this world. It was God's creation. It was used by God for His purposes. It was not only availed of by the citizens of God's city but was also intended by God to give compelling example to them of what efforts they should make in their striving for something greater and something higher.

Out of that world and what good it had to offer, Christians should take the "spoils of the Egyptians" and should make them their own. They should profit from secular philosophy (which in its own way was a kind of revelation); they should learn from secular history (which in its own way threw prophetic light upon the future).

Absolutely, if things were to be judged only by the canon of the service and worship of the true God, what the Hebrews achieved in their temporal history, the Greeks in their academies, and the Romans in the virtues of their worthies, was evil. For evil was merely not-to-do-that-service-and-give-that-worship. In this way what looked like virtue was really splendid vice. But *relatively*, or in our ordinary way of speaking, all these things were good and should be used by Christianity. Christianity had changed superficially, was no longer the religion of a few fishermen, was in fact the religion of an Empire accepting its intellectual responsibility. This superficial change wrought through assimilation, absorption, reaction and, it might be, rejection was the law of its life. The Leviathan that challenges now is greater than it has ever been. The weapons must ever be the same.

Almost the only thing that could not be accepted from Rome was her official religion, polytheism. Insofar as the *City of God* is against anything, it is radically against that. It is unfortunate that Augustine in placing the positive part of his argument in the final twelve books and the negative in the first ten, gives the impression that he is opposed to Rome and Greek philosophy. If he had stated the basis of his positive doctrine first, it would be seen that his attitude to Rome and Greece and his general outlook is positive.

Augustine's message for Christianity in an expanding and secular world, if judged by the *City of God*, would be to seek the good in what is secular, to seek the good in other cultures, to adopt a constructive and sympathetic attitude to State and world. Christians sometimes give the impression that they lack confidence in God's providence and the goodness of creation. Sometimes too they show little evidence of Christian hope. Without that confidence and that hope they bring less than they should to a world in great need and dire distress.

Part I of this lecture is intended to place the *City of God* in its full context and describe (in Augustine's own words) its contents and order. Part II, being in three divisions, follows the divisions of the *City of God* itself, but in reverse order. The notes do not give a full bibliography, but enable one to find it. References to the *City of God* throughout are by book and chapter. References to the *Confessions* and other works are by book and section. Longer extracts from the *City of God*, unless otherwise indicated, are from the translation in the series *Fathers of the Church*, New York. In certain ways this lecture as a whole, but especially Part II, B, owes much to a technical work, *Porphyry's Philosophy from Oracles in Augustine*, prepared at the Institute for Advanced Study, Princeton, New Jersey, and published by Etudes Augustiniennes, Paris, 1959.

Contents

Background to the
City of God

I

The Relevant Historical Situation

1

Augustine, born and reared in Roman North Africa in the second half of the fourth century, grew up in an Empire that was in evident decline. Rome's marble city, her invincible army, her wide-flung administration, her riches garnered from every corner of the world, but above all her spirit and very heart were failing. The fatal blow came quickly. On a day in August in A.D. 410, Alaric with his Christian-Arian Goths sacked the great city that had not known violation by a foreign enemy for eight hundred years.

One does not need much imagination or sensibility to understand how symbolic of impending doom Rome's fall might appear to be. Even two years afterward St. Jerome was still so affected by it that he could not dictate his commentary on Ezechiel. He

3

had, he complained, lost the memory of his own name and could but remain silent, knowing that it was a time to weep: with Rome had perished the human race. This was the reaction of a Christian—but, it should be added, an emotional Christian. Another Christian, Orosius, a contemporary of the event and the chief source of information on the sack of Rome, judges soberly that the damage to the city was not great.

It is well to bear in mind that, while the sack lasted but three days and was marked by the relative clemency of the conquerors, the overthrowing of the official Roman religion, a form of polytheism, had been prolonged, bitter, and serious in its consequences. From the time of Constantine onward there had been a succession of edicts against paganism, twenty of them in the last twenty years of the fourth century, and as many as four in the last year of that century, as if it had been determined that with the century paganism should pass from the Empire forever: idols were to be dethroned; temples to be laicized; judges were to be supervised in the enforcement of the edicts; and bishops were to report any laxity in the carrying out of these instructions.

There had, of course, been opposition to such a policy. An instance of this can be seen in the short-lived respite of the reign of Julian the Apostate (361–363). The symbolical event, however, in this spiritual struggle is usually seen in the confrontation of Symmachus, the Prefect of Rome and the outstanding professed pagan of his day, with St. Ambrose of Milan on the question of the Altar of Victory in 384.

4

The great goddess Victory, associated with Jupiter (chief of the Roman gods), and with Mars (god of war), worshiped by the army (the instrument of Rome's dominion), and intimately related to the felicity of the emperor, had been furnished with an altar, the Altar of Victory, within the very Senate House itself of Rome. There she had stood, presiding over the prosperity of Rome, an earnest and an omen of continuing success. This altar had been removed by Constantius, the father of Constantine, replaced by the pagans in due course, removed again under Gratian in 382, replaced for a brief period by Eugenius (392–394), and perhaps on a final occasion by Stilicho, who died in disgrace in 408.

Of Augustine's acquaintance with one of the protagonists, St. Ambrose, in the symbolical confrontation on the Altar of Victory, it will not be necessary to say anything here.[1] On the other hand we should remember that, when Augustine came to teach Rhetoric in Carthage in 374 and had some acquaintance with official circles there, Symmachus was not only in residence as proconsul of Africa but had also been one of the most successful rhetors of his time. It is not unlikely that they met then, but in any case Symmachus knew of Augustine at least later in Rome; for it was he, the most prominent pagan of his day, who recommended Augustine for appointment to the office of Master of Rhetoric at the Imperial Court, then at Milan, the See of St. Ambrose. It is well to pause and reflect on the significance that this situation, pregnant as it was to be, must have had for Augustine. Here he was in Milan, a non-Christian as

5

yet, recommended by the champion of the pagans—perhaps for the very reason, among others, that Augustine was not a Christian—at a court subject to the influence of the champion of the Christians. Augustine arrived in Milan in the autumn of 384, only a month or two after the dispute on the Altar of Victory.

Symmachus's part in the affair is represented by a petition for the restoration of the altar, removed, as we have seen, in 382. This petition is extant.[2] As Prefect of the city of Rome and Pontifex Maximus, he stressed the necessity for prudence: no one knew the final secret explanation of Rome's prosperity; it was therefore unwise not to preserve the institutions that had presided over her success; it was perilous to disown them for something new. He brought Rome herself forward to plead her cause: she is old; she has no desire to change her pieties; her religion has civilized the world, driven the Gauls from the Capitol and Hannibal from the city.

St. Ambrose, however, was a doughty opponent, as his domination of the Arian Empress Justina in 385–386 and of the Emperor Theodosius (with the imposition of a public penance in 390) was soon to show. His argument[3] was that the valor and virtues of the Romans themselves were sufficient explanation of their successes. Was it not foolish to pretend to believe that the Empire depended on some "power" that one must imagine but could not see? To restrict the future through reverence for the mere past was to retard progress and civilization. Christianity had, moreover, a positive contribution to make: it held

6

truth and salvation, while polytheism led to perdition and error.

The Christian cause prevailed, and paganism was clearly and definitely, if not finally, defeated. Prudentius, the Christian poet, describes[4] how the Senate in plenary session formally banished Jupiter and the other gods in favor of the Christian God. The senators, many of whom were known to be dissembling, yielded to mounting public approbation of Christianity and abandoned for monotheism the gods of their forefathers. They made haste to disown their ancient pride, submit to baptism, and pay reverence at the tombs of the Christian martyrs.

The ordinary people were not slow to show their satisfaction, and soon the temples were molding in desolation. Theodosius in his time was relentless in his enforcement of the edicts against polytheism throughout the Empire, and particularly those against sacrifice to the gods. Some indeed in their zeal, fearing that shrines that were merely empty might one day be restored, hastened to destroy the temples themselves, some of them splendid edifices. A few of them were converted to Christian use, the most famous of these being the Pantheon, the temple in Rome of all the gods, which to this day stands as it ever stood.

The decrees of Theodosius, however, reached further even than destruction of the buildings. Sacrifice to idols and divination by inspection of entrails—the commonplaces of public life in Rome—were declared to be high treason and were to be punished by death. Even the most trivial trafficking in garlands and

7

libations was suspected and became liable to fines and confiscation of property.

The collapse of polytheism was in the end sudden, universal within the Empire, and absolute. Its absurdity as a religious system had long before been accepted by the intelligent. Now the wholesale assault on buildings and institutions with evident impunity and no retaliation from the ousted and enfeebled gods delivered the masses from any feelings of fear or obligation. The dismemberment of the great god Serapis at Alexandria met with no revenge in either the death of a Christian or the refusal of the Nile to grant its annual and blessed inundation. Truly the gods had lost, and Christ had won:

> *Et dubitamus adhuc Romam, tibi, Christe, dicatam*
> *In leges transisse tuas?*[5]

Augustine was by his very circumstances a close observer of this stupendous transformation. As he was torn between the loyalties he owed first to Symmachus and then to St. Ambrose, so his feelings and thoughts were divided between sympathy for the Rome that was and the vision of a Christian future. Nevertheless his evident delight, for example, at the destruction of the pagan temples at Carthage by Jovius and Gaudentius,[6] and his approval of even punishment by death for pagan sacrificing,[7] leave no doubt, if doubt were possible, where his final loyalty lay. He was not unaware that the recent desertion en masse from an enervated polytheism meant that there were Christians, even many Christians, who had yielded to Christ for unworthy motives—to save their lives or canvass official support for their careers and ambitions—but for all that he felt an overflowing happiness in the visible victory of the Christians.

It is hardly surprising, then, if Augustine's distress at the sack of Rome in 410 was not only much less pronounced than that of St. Jerome but was compensated for by a greater optimism. If the pagan historians Zosimus and Rutilius Namatianus, writing of the period, say not a word of the disaster—possibly because they did not find it an attractive topic—we can understand that Augustine's fondness for a theme, about which he was sometimes twitted, was prompted more by its wider significance, as marking a stage in the conflict between Christianity and paganism, than by any preoccupation with the material decline and fall of Rome. The theme was with him an old one, even before the sack of Rome.

The question was, however, raised for him directly by a Christian official in Africa, Marcellinus—to whom in fact the *City of God* is addressed—in a letter (136) in the year 412, the year before Augustine began his greatest book. Marcellinus mentioned the view put forward by some of his friends that the miracles wrought by Apollonius and Apuleius were greater than those of Christianity. He asked how, if God had been satisfied with the type of sacrifice described in the Old Testament, He could, without changing (which in God is impossible), be dissatisfied with it in the New? Finally there arose the problem of why it was that the Empire appeared to decline when it came to be governed by princes that had forsaken the old, tried,

9

McAULEY LIBRARY
MT. MERCY COLLEGE
Cedar Rapids, Iowa 52402

religion and embraced a new one that inculcated precepts of toleration of offenses and submission to injury. This did not seem to go well with the interests of Empire.

One should note carefully that, although this letter was written about two years after the sack of Rome, and purported to give the views and complaints of pagans, there is not one word about the event in question, but rather the whole emphasis is on miracles, sacrifices, and religion as causes or explanations of success in Empire or failure.

Augustine replied in a letter to a friend of Marcellinus (137) and in a further one to Marcellinus himself (138). The themes of these two letters foreshadow very clearly themes of the *City of God*, and some of them must be briefly mentioned: the Saviour came when the time was ripe for His coming; that coming was foretold not only by the prophets but also by secular philosophers and poets; the true Mediator delivered man from the false mediators, the demons; Christ superseded Moses, who was greater than any pagan; the truth of Christianity is seen in its fulfillment of prophecy and its confirmation by miracles; the world is declining and is in its last age; Christians are multiplying everywhere and await the eternal happiness of the heavenly city (*aeternam ciuitatis coelestis felicitatem* [137]).

Letter 138 concentrates more on the question of religion and Empire: the gods of polytheism, being by definition many, were discordant and inimical to concord, which was the constituting element of the (Roman) State; this discord issued in civil wars; the gods favor the evils that corrupt men; Christianity, on the contrary, makes men better as soldiers, better as parents, and better as children, better as masters and better as slaves, better as princes, better as judges, better as taxpayers and better as taxgatherers—in short, Christianity was the great salvation for the State; it goes, however, beyond this life below and the harmony of the State, and provides entry to eternal salvation and the heavenly and divine republic of a certain eternal people (*sempiterni cuiusdam populi coelestem diuinamque rempublicam*); the splendid success of the Romans, achieved without the true religion, is perfected in their becoming citizens of another city (*ciues alterius ciuitatis*). The letter goes on to insist that the pagan gods are less powerful than even Apollonius or Apuleius; the demons caused damage to the State and aroused hostility to Christianity; prosperity with the worship of the true God was seen in the temporal history of the Hebrews, whose dispersal, even as enemies of Christianity, aided its spread; the miracles of Christianity are incomparably superior to any others.

Augustine ends this second letter by admitting that he has not managed to treat of all the points that he would wish. If Marcellinus writes for more, he will make it his business to reply either in a letter or in a book (*uel epistolis uel libris*).

In the event he wrote a book for Marcellinus. It was the *City of God*, was begun in 413, the following year, and it deals with essentially the same topics and with the same attitudes.

Anticipations of the Theme in Augustine

2

Of the last stages in the conflict between polytheism and Christian monotheism, Augustine could not but have been conscious, at least from the time of his being recommended by Symmachus to Milan, where he encountered St. Ambrose. What happened to himself in 386, when he was converted, represented in his own regard a victory for Christianity. It would not be surprising, then, if in the earliest compositions of Augustine there were adumbrations and preliminary formulations of what was later the dominating theme of the *City of God*.

A study has been made of the various anticipations in Augustine of this later theme;[8] but here we shall confine ourselves to a very few only, and these from his first extant works, which reflect very strongly his own personal experiences at the time of his conversion.

Our purpose is to show how the main theme of the *City of God* had already taken on a special significance for him as he reflected upon the pattern of his own life. Even at that stage he had begun to think that what was true for him was true for mankind at large.

We must ourselves at this point anticipate in assuming that the dominating theme of the *City of God* is salvation and the means to it: the worship of the one true God, involving the rejection of all false gods.

Whereas salvation in the *City of God* is represented by citizenship in a city *(ciuitas)*—an image explicitly taken from the Scriptures—it is in the earliest formulations represented as arriving at harbor *(portus)*, or at the fatherland *(patria)*, or being upon the way *(uia)*. These images are, of course, borrowed from the stock in trade of philosophy, particularly Platonic philosophy, in its eschatological aspects. Other variants used by Augustine at this time are the land of desire *(optatissima terra)*, the land of happiness *(beatae uitae regionem solumque)*, the happy land *(terra beata)*, and the shining home *(luculentam domum)*.

The first few pages of Augustine's first extant work, the *Contra Academicos*, written after his conversion in 386, speak of the harbor of wisdom *(portus sapientiae)*, to which Providence, making use of misfortune that seems to be but evil, brings us. Special emphasis is laid upon the irrelevance and instability of temporal prosperity. Here Augustine alludes directly not only to the apparent misfortunes of the person to whom the book is addressed, but to his own: prosperity had almost entrapped him, but he had been compelled by illness to give up his profession and betake himself to philosophy, which, as the work makes clear, means philosophy subject to the authority of Christ (III. 43). One can suppose that Augustine's views, on the irrelevance of prosperity and the use made by Providence of misfortune, might be applied by him to the Empire as much as to mankind in general or himself and his friend.

The image of the harbor is used again in the first five sections of the *De Beata Vita*, composed at the same time as the previous work. The major image here, however, is the land of desire. There are two ways to this land, both across a sea. One is the way of reason, which, possible only for the few, brings men to the harbor of philosophy, which is the harbor of the land of desire. The other way is the way of Providence which uses the storms of adversity to bring men, resist and wander in ignorance and folly as they may, to the same harbor. Those who are apparently most successful in life have need of the greatest storms. Some are brought to sanity, however, by the reading of books written by the learned and the wise. And some make their way to the fatherland partly by their own use of reason, and partly by providential adversity.

One great hazard threatens all who approach the harbor—a high mountain in front of the harbor itself. It is so enticing that it lures to it not only those approaching the harbor, but even some that had already been in the harbor. The people living on this mountain are full of conceit, and fear that others might share their glory; hence they impress on those approaching the difficulty, because of submerged rocks, of joining themselves and are happy to advise them how they can get to the land of desire. In this way they are themselves destroyed within sight of the shining home.

Finally—a most important point—the harbor is wide, and one may still fail to put ashore and so not achieve one's goal.

There are significant anticipations of the *City of God* here. The very term "citizens" (*ciues*) is used, and the phrase "on pilgrimage from their fatherland" (*a sua patria peregrinari*) is that characteristically applied in the later work to the citizens of the heavenly city in their life on earth. The illusions of prosperity and the transcendent role of Providence in its use of adversity are here fully emphasized. Of particular significance, however, is the special mention of the envious and proud, who help others to safety, but are themselves destroyed within sight of the fatherland. This, of course, must refer especially to certain Neoplatonists, who approached Christianity, helped others to become Christians, but rejected Christianity themselves. It is to be noted that not all mankind reach the harbor, and those who are there may still be lost: so too might Christians fail to persevere.

What is of particular interest for us here is Augustine's explicit relation of this theme and image to the circumstances of his own life at the time. Here indeed he gives a summary autobiography, parallel to that given in the *Contra Academicos* (II. 4f.), and later to be expanded in the *Confessions*. It is clear that the theme, as set out in the *De Beata Vita*, is inspired by his own life: the providential use of illness, the effect of reading certain books (a very precise detail that he repeats and applies without hesitation to other men), his own part use of reason and part guidance by Providence, the illusions of prosperity, and the help of the proud Neoplatonists, who did not benefit from their own wisdom.

In short we have here the opportunity of seeing how the theme of the *City of God* is revealed by himself as constructed from the details of his own conversion. To put it another way, the *City of God* is the application of the *Confessions* to the history of mankind. The inspiration of Augustine's themes is in his life.

The image of the way (*uia*) is found first in Augustine in, again, the *Contra Academicos* (III. 34). Here we are given the story of two men traveling to the same destination, one of whom has too much and the other too little credulity. At a crossroads they meet a humble shepherd whose directions the one accepts without question and proceeds to follow. The other ridicules such credulity and does not move. By the time an elegant gentleman came along on horseback he had found his waiting tedious, and accordingly acted upon the directions now given, although he did not accept them as necessarily true and they conflicted with those given by the shepherd. In the event he got lost in the woods and trackless mountains—for the horseman was an impostor—while his companion was resting at his destination.

The source of this image may have been epistemological, but Augustine explicitly refers its use here to the deeds and behavior of men (*ipsa facta hominum et mores considerare coepi*). Philosophers and those interested in religion had done so before him, and amongst those was one especially well known to himself, Porphyry. Porphyry's search for a universal way to salvation and his rejection of Christ as that way is the high point of the tenth book of the *City of God* and, perhaps, of the work as a whole. Although Augustine's use of the image of the way is undoubtedly at a later stage influenced by Moses' leading of his followers to the promised land and by the description of the Magi's return by another way into their own country, his treatment of it in the *Confessions* (VII. 26f.) and the *De Trinitate* (IV. 13ff.) is basically the same as here in the *Contra Academicos* and later in the *City of God* (X. 32): the contrasting attitudes of the proud and the humble, the simple and credulous, and the pretentious impostor. The *Confessions* mark the point well: "I might discern and distinguish between presumption and confession, between those who saw whither they were to go, yet saw not the way, and the way that leadeth not to behold only but to dwell in the beatific country. For it is one thing to see the land of peace, and to find no way thither; and in vain to essay through ways impassable, opposed and beset by fugitives and deserters, and another to keep on the way that leads thither" (translation by Edward Pusey in Everyman's Library).

Unlike those in the image of the harbor in the *De Beata Vita*, the Neoplatonists are here represented as seeking direction but being deceived. Both images complete the treatment of them in the *City of God* where they are shown as helping toward the truth, but also as being deceived.

It will not be necessary for our purpose to linger further on other anticipations of the main theme of the *City of God*. The clearest and fullest is to be found in the *De Vera Religione* (cf. 48ff.) which was begun at the same time as the works we have been discussing, but was not finished until four years later in 390. Inasmuch as the *City of God* is a discussion of religion (*disputatio religionis*), both works share the same topic. The *De Moribus Ecclesiae Catholicae*, written in 388–390, has this striking passage on the "way," which is, at the same time, a summary statement of one aspect and much of the contents of the *City of God*: "the way which God built for us in the segregation of the Patriarchs, the bond of the Law, the foretelling of the Prophets, the sacrament of the Man assumed, the testimony of the Apostles, the blood of the martyrs and the entering into possession of the gentiles. Let us heed the oracles (of Scripture) and submit our puny reasonings to divine inspiration" (I. 11f.). Here the *gradual* revelation of the way is emphasized. Finally the *De Catechizandis Rudibus*, written in 399, speaks plainly of two cities, one the devil's, the other Christ's.

What we have wanted to stress was not so much the anticipation of the theme of the *City of God*, thereby showing that it was not necessarily dependent upon Alaric's sack of Rome, but even more the root-

18

ing of that theme in Augustine's own experience. This will be found to be of use in the understanding of the theme as it was later set forth. As Providence had used adversity to help him, so does Providence dominate the life of every man and every Empire. This might be a banal teaching of a philosophical school, but for Augustine it was also a personal realization, and so it tended to color and affect all his thoughts and all his theories. Implicit in all this is some regret for that prosperity from which Providence tears us; but there is compensation in the assurance afforded by the fulfillment of prophecies, the miracles of the saints, and the conversion of the multitudes. Even at the temporal level an Empire must benefit from the improved moral character of its citizens, once they were Christians.

If, then, there is sorrow and regret for the past, there is also joy for the future; and if there is somber pessimism, there is also unbounded hope. The thoughts and images that Augustine uses reflect the experience and life of an artist, the complicated tension of whose anxious spirit reveals to us his large humanity and ardent sensibility.

Augustine's Descriptions of the Book

3

M. H. I. Marrou, one of the greatest Augustinian scholars of our day, while rightly insisting that salvation is the central drama of the *City of God*, chides[9] us for persisting in the effort to find there the answers to many problems: the rights and duties of the State, the relations of Church and State, the possibility of a Kingdom of God on earth, the explanation of the Reformation, the transmission of Platonism, a philosophy of history, a theology of history—and much else besides. He points to Gilson's book, *Les métamorphoses de la Cité de Dieu* (Paris, 1952), as a veritable inventory of these "caricatures" of the true subject of Augustine's work.

With some of these not unfairly labeled "caricatures" we shall deal in appropriate places. It will be useful at this stage, however, to put the reader in immediate contact with Augustine's own descriptions of his book. Whether he was writing a letter to the priest Firmus,[10] or engaged in the opening chapters of certain stages of the work, or reviewing it as a whole when he came to publish his *Retractations*, his general outline and description are both accurate and unvarying. Here we shall give without comment his over-all description in the *Retractations*, followed by his explanations at various important points of the book as it proceeded.

Retractations (II. 69) 426–427.

In the meantime Rome had been swept by an invasion of the Goths under the leadership of King Alaric and the impact of a great disaster; and the worshippers of the many false gods, to whom we commonly give the name of pagans, attempting to attribute this visitation to the Christian religion, began more sharply and more bitterly than usual to blaspheme the true God. Burning with the zeal of God's house, I decided to write against their blasphemies and errors the books on *The City of God*. This work engaged me for some years because many other matters intervened that I could not conscientiously postpone, and kept me busy completing them first. At last, however, this huge work on *The City of God* was brought to a conclusion in twenty-two books.

The *first five* books *refute* those whose interest in *the welfare of mankind* is bound up with the belief that this *depends on the worship of the many gods* whom the pagans were wont to worship, and who maintain that the misfortunes in question owe their existence and magnitude to the prohibition of that worship. The *next five* books, again, *are an answer to* such as, though they admit

21

that mortal men were never in the past spared such misfortunes nor will be in the future, and that ill fortune is sometimes greater, sometimes less as it affects different regions, eras or individuals, yet maintain that *the worship of many gods, in which sacrifices are made to them, is advantageous because of the life that will be ours after death.* In these ten books, then, are refuted those two false notions that are contrary to the Christian religion.

But lest someone reply that we have only argued against the opinions of others but have not stated our own, this is attended to in *the second part* of this work, which *comprises twelve books.* When need arises, however, our own position is also stated in the first ten books, and opposing views are also refuted in the twelve later books.

Of these twelve succeeding books, *the first four* contain the *origin of the two cities, the one of God, the other of this world; the second four, their* course or *progress; the* third and *last four, their appointed ends.* And so all twenty-two books, though they dealt with *both cities,* yet took their *title from the better,* with the result that they were called by preference *The City of God.* [Translation by G. E. McCracken in the Loeb Series, Vol. I, pp. 3-5. Italics added.]

The text of the *City of God* itself is furnished with a set of headings for every chapter of the work. This goes back to medieval times and is sometimes attributed to Augustine himself or said to have been composed on his instructions. A perusal of it will acquaint the reader with the actual matter of the work.

Augustine reviews the progress of the work at special junctures—such as Books II. 2; III. 1; IV. 1-2; VI. Preface and 1; XI. 1; XII. 1; XVIII. 1. Of these a few are as follows:

Book VI. *Preface and* 1

In the five preceding Books, I have, I hope, sufficiently refuted those who think that many gods are to be venerated and worshiped . . . in order to gain advantages for this mortal life and men's temporal affairs . . . which (worship) is due to the true God alone. Christian truth makes clear that these gods are false, that they are useless idols, or unclean spirits, or dangerous demons, or, at best, mere creatures and not the Creator.

. . . My next purpose, then . . . will be the refutation and instruction of those who hold that the gods of the pagans, which Christianity rejects, are to be worshiped . . . with a view to life after death. The starting point . . . will be the revealed truth (*ueridico oraculo*) of the holy psalm. . . .

Book XI. 1

The expression, "City of God," which I have been using is justified by that Scripture whose divine authority puts it above the literature of all other people and brings under its sway every type of human genius . . . not by some casual intellectual reaction, but by a disposition of Divine Providence. For, in this Scripture, we read: "Glorious things are said of thee, O city of God" [*Ps.* 86.3. Other references to 'city of God' in the Psalms follow.] . . .

Through these and similar passages too numerous to quote, we learn of the existence of a City of God whose Founder has inspired us with a love and longing to become its citizens. The inhabitants of the earthly city who prefer their own gods to the Founder of the holy City do not realize that He is the God of gods—though not, of course, of those false, wicked and proud gods who, because they have been deprived of that unchangeable light which was meant for all, are reduced to a pitiful power and, therefore, are eager for some sort of influence and demand divine honors . . . [but] of those reverent and holy gods who prefer to obey and worship one God rather than to have many others . . . worshiping them.

. . . Now . . . realizing what is expected of me . . . to discuss . . . the origin, history, and destiny of the respective cities . . . which . . . are at present inextricably intermingled (*in hoc interim saeculo perplexas quodam modo inuicemque permixtas*) . . . first, I shall explain how these two cities originated when the angels took opposing sides (*in angelorum diuersitate*).

Book XII. 1

. . . we must now proceed to the creation of men and see the beginning of the cities so far as it concerns the kind of rational creatures who are mortal. First, . . . there is no real difficulty or impropriety in speaking of a single society composed of both men and angels . . . therefore, it is right to say that there are not four cities or societies . . . but only two, one of them made up of the good—both angels and men—and the other of those who are evil.

There is no reason to doubt that the contrary dispositions . . . among these good and bad angels are due, not to different natures and origins, for God the Author and Creator of all substances has created them both, but to the dissimilar choices and desires of these angels themselves. Some, remaining faithful to God, the common good of all, have lived in the enjoyment of His eternity, truth, and love, while others, preferring the enjoyment of their own power, as though they were their own good, departed from the higher good and common blessedness for all and turned to goods of their own choosing . . . preferring . . . pride to . . . eternity, the craftiness of vanity to the certainty of truth, and the turmoil of dissension to the

24

union of love . . . they became proud, deceitful, and envious.

Since the happiness of all angels consists in union with God (*adhaerere Deo*), it follows that their unhappiness must be found in the very contrary, that is, in not adhering to God.

Book XV. 1

. . . I think I have said enough on the really great and difficult problems concerning the origin of the world, the soul, and the human race. In regard to mankind I have made a division . . . those who live according to man . . . those who live according to God. And . . . in a deeper sense, we may speak of two cities or two human societies, the destiny of the one being an eternal kingdom under God while the doom of the other is eternal punishment along with the Devil. (*In duo genera distribuimus, unum eorum, qui secundum hominem, alterum eorum, qui secundum Deum uiuunt; quas etiam mystice appellamus ciuitates duas, hoc est duas societates hominum, quarum est una quae praedestinata est in aeternum regnare cum Deo, altera aeternum supplicium subire cum diabolo.*)

Of the final consummation of the two cities I shall have to speak later. Of their original cause among the angels whose number no man knows and then in the first two human beings, I have already spoken. . . . therefore, I must deal with the course of the history of the two cities from the time when children were born to the first couple until the day when men shall beget no more . . . as distinguished from their original cause and final consummation, I mean the whole time of world history in which men are born and take the place of those who die and depart.

Now, the first man born of the two parents of the

human race was Cain. He belonged to the city of man. The next born was Abel, and he was of the City of God. We all experience as individuals what the Apostle says: "It is not the spiritual that comes first, but the physical, and then the spiritual." The fact is that every individual springs from a condemned stock and, because of Adam, must be first cankered and carnal, only later to become sound and spiritual by the process of rebirth in Christ. So, too, with the human race as a whole, as soon as human birth and death began the historical course of the two cities, the first to be born was a citizen of this world and only later came the one who was an alien in the city of men but at home in the City of God, a man predestined by grace and elected by grace. By grace an alien on earth, by grace he was a citizen of heaven (*isto peregrinus in saeculo et pertinens ad ciuitatem Dei, gratia praedestinatus gratia electus, gratia peregrinus deorsum gratia ciuis sursum*).

"For as for his birth, it was out of the same corrupted mass that was condemned from the beginning (*en ladem massa quae originaliter est tota damnata*); but God could make "from the same mass one vessel for honorable, another for ignoble use." The first vessel to be made was "for ignoble use." Only later was there made a vessel for honorable use (*Rom.* 9. 21)....as I have said, with the individual . . . comes the clay that is only fit to be thrown away, with which we must begin, but in which we need not remain. Afterwards comes what is fit for use, that into which we can be gradually molded and in which, when molded, we may remain. This does not mean that every one who is wicked is to become good, but that no one becomes good who was not once wicked. . . .

Now, it is recorded of Cain that he built a city, while Abel . . . a pilgrim on earth, built none. For, the true City of the saints is in heaven, though here on earth it produces citizens in whom it wanders as on a pilgrimage through time looking for the Kingdom of eternity. When that day comes it will gather together all those who, rising in their bodies, shall have that Kingdom given to them in which, along with their Prince, the King of Eternity, they shall reign for ever and ever (*superna est enim sanctorum ciuitas, quamuis hic pariat ciues, in quibus peregrinatur, donec regni eius tempus adueniat, cum congregatura est omnes in suis corporibus resurgentes, quando eis promissum dabitur regnum, ubi cum principe rege saeculorum sine ullo temporis fine regnabunt*).

Book XXII. 30

[This, the last chapter of the *City of God*, gives a summary of Augustine's view of the history of mankind in the past and for the future.]

There is a clear indication of this final Sabbath if we take the seven ages of world history as being "days" and calculate in accordance with the data furnished by the Scriptures. The first age or day is that from Adam to the flood; the second, from the flood to Abraham . . . not identical in length of time, but in each there were ten generations. Then follow the three ages, each consisting of fourteen generations, as recorded in the Gospel of St. Matthew . . . to Christ's nativity. . . . Thus, we have five ages. The sixth is the one in which we now are . . . an age not to be measured by any precise number . . . since we are told: "It is not for you to know the times or dates which the Father has fixed by his own authority" (*Acts* 1. 7). After this "day," God will rest on the "seventh day," in the sense that God will make us, who are to be this seventh day, rest in Him.

. . . this "seventh day" will be our Sabbath and . . .

27

will end in no evening, but only in the Lord's day—that eighth and eternal day which dawned when Christ's resurrection heralded an eternal rest both for the spirit and for the body. On that day we shall rest and see, see and love, love and praise. . . .

The *City of God:*
Charter of Christendom

II

Preliminary Note on the Structure
of the *City of God*

There are a few preliminary observations one should make about the structure of the *City of God*. The final twelve books deal in the main with the history of time and eternity as given in the Bible, which is of Jewish provenance. Of the first ten books the second five deal mainly with Greek philosophy, more particularly Platonism, and especially with the Neoplatonists Plotinus and Porphyry—with lengthy consideration of the views of the latter. The first five books deal in the main with the polytheism of Rome, with special reference to Varro. Here are the three great centers of the work: the Bible, Greece, and Rome. Augustine himself draws attention to this most explicitly in one of the most dramatic sections of the work (XIX. 22):

"Who is this God of yours, and how do we know that the Romans were obliged to adore Him with sacrifices to the exclusion of other gods?" One must be blind indeed to be asking at this late date who our God is! He is the God whose Prophets foretold things we see realized under our very eyes. He is the God who gave the reply to Abraham: "In thy seed shall all the nations of the earth be blessed" (*Gen.* 22. 18) . . . this promise has been made good in Christ, born in the flesh of Abraham's seed—a fulfillment which those who have remained opposed to Christ's name know so well, though they like it so little. He is the God whose Spirit spoke through Prophets whose predictions are now realized in our visibly world-wide Church and which I quoted in previous Books. He is the God whom Varro, the most learned of Romans, thought was Jupiter, however little he grasped the import of his words. It is at least worth mentioning that a man of his learning was unable to think of our God as despicable or non-existent. . . . Varro identified Him with his own conception of the supreme deity.

Finally, our God is the one whom Porphyry, most learned of philosophers and bitter enemy of Christianity, admits to be a great God, and this on the strength of pagan oracles.

The first sentence in this excerpt indicates Augustine's standpoint in the whole of his inquiry: the Roman world (cf. III. 1). His attitude is not negative; on the contrary he is concerned for that world's future. Rome was to bring together within herself the revelation in the Bible, the wisdom of Greek philosophy, and what was good in her own tradition. Augustine is fully conscious of the fusion of the elements that in fact went to make up the civilization of the West that has endured to this day. In this sense his *City of God* is a, if not the, Charter of Christendom, and in this lies its greatest significance.

The Bible, Greek philosophy, Roman speculation on religion all pointed to one God, the God of the Hebrews. This God should now be accepted as the God of Rome. The prophecies in their fulfillment, and the Church in its extension, its martyrs, and its miracles, left no doubt possible on this. The aspirations of Hebrews, Greeks, and Romans were to be fulfilled in a Christian Rome. The Christian Era, the *tempora Christiana,* was already a reality. Even if some evils endured, it was a blessed reality.

Augustine may have come to these pregnant views through reading or argument; but it is most unlikely that once again his own personal experience did not influence him here also. His was a life led in a Roman environment, based on Roman education, drawing importantly upon Greek philosophy at a time most critical to his development, and resting in the main after his conversion on the Christian Scriptures. His *Confessions* not merely testify to this in contents: in very form they too describe a Roman's background and education (I–VII. 12), the contribution of Greek philosophy (VII. 13–IX), and life according to the Christian revelation. In particular the last three books of the *Confessions* cover in part the same ground as is later covered in the fuller and richer canvas of the last twelve books of the *City of God.*

There are rudimentary traces of the same progress from Rome to Greece to the Scriptures in others of Augustine's works. The *Contra Academicos* proceeds from Cicero to the *schola Plotini*, but puts the authority of Christ above that again (III. 43). The preface to the *De Beata Vita*, with which we have already dealt, implies a similar progression. The contemporary *De Ordine* in its turn discusses more explicitly (II. 25–54) a system of education based on the same lines.

In the pages that follow we shall take our cue from Augustine and consider the *City of God* from the three angles indicated by himself: its interpretation of the Bible; its attitude to Greek philosophy, in effect to Platonism, or more precisely Neoplatonism; and its attitude to Rome.

The Bible

A

Augustine's first and final evidence on any point in the *City of God* is the declaration of the Scriptures: "We ought first to place the divine testimonies as it were in the foundation of the building" (XX. I). In his view the authority of Scripture is the most exalted, and is preeminent over everything else whatsoever (XI. I).

This is not an idle declaration; with it corresponds Augustine's practice. The whole approach of the book is from the viewpoint of the Scriptures, and the matter of the larger second part is, in addition, taken from the Bible.

Such confidence, Augustine believed, was justified by the fulfillment of its prophecies, by the miracles of Christianity, and by the flocking, as it seemed, of all mankind to the feet of Christ. Revelation had been gradual, proceeding more slowly in the beginning, becoming much clearer in the election of Abraham, and finally manifested in the coming of the Saviour. Among the many passages[11] dealing with this theme, a few might be considered representative, of which one will be taken from outside the *City of God*:

I shall begin the description of His (God's) deeds among men from (the time of) Abraham. For to him a manifest promise was made through an angelic oracle (*angelicum oraculum*), which we now see being fulfilled. For to him it was said: "In your seed shall all the nations be blessed" (*Gen.* XXII. 18): from whose seed is the people of Israel, whence the Virgin Mary, who bore Christ, in whom are blessed all the nations let those now dare to deny who can. And not in the Christian era, but long before, was that predicted which is being fulfilled by Christians: "to Thee shall the nations come from the end of the earth" (*Jer.* XVI. 19). Behold now it is happening; behold the nations are now coming to Christ from the end of the earth, repeating these words and breaking idols." [*De Consensu Euangelistarum* I. 39f. 400 A.D.]

. . . these things were not done and recorded without some prefiguring of what was to come and . . . they are to be referred only to Christ and His Church, which is the City of God. . . . [XVI. 2] . . . it is in these oracles (*oracula*) (to Abraham) that the utterances of our God, Who is the true God, begin to have a clearer reference to the chosen people. . . . [XVI. 30] . . . of all the truths they preached the chief is this: that Christ rose from the dead and was the first to reveal that immortality of resurrection in the flesh. . . . [XXII. 10]

36

Among the miracles used to confirm Scripture the one which was preeminent was Christ's resurrection (XXII. 10). This, as we shall see, was of special significance in Augustine's work.

It will have been noticed that in the quotations just given the Scriptures are referred to as oracles. This is not otiose or an accident: it is frequent and deliberate throughout the *City of God*. There are, for example, a dozen instances of it in Books XVI–XVIII. The reason for this is not far to seek. Augustine, in confronting a book of Porphyry's entitled *Philosophy from Oracles*,[12] was facing pagan oracles of considerable repute. These oracles he repudiated—but not so as to deny that they might convey some truth. God's revelation was not confined *solely* to Scripture, and Augustine was ready to recognize that God might reveal His truth as He pleased. The God we worship chose certain spirits and gave them the power of foresight, and through them He makes prophecies (VII. 30).

His confident contention, however, was that the oracles of the Christian Scriptures were not few and obscure as were those of the pagans (XIX. 23). The foreknowledge God gave even to demons was unsure, and the demons themselves could be deceived (IX. 22). This could not be said of the Scriptures, which were oracles many and clear.

The consideration of the Scriptures from this angle, that is, in contrast with and as superior to the oracles of Porphyry, lends special significance to Augustine's treatment of his problem in this way. Since his declared doughtiest opponent was Porphyry, he would engage him not only directly in argument but also in the whole technique of his work.

Apart from Augustine's confident recourse to Scripture for truth and his assurance of its evident superiority over pagan oracles, there is one other point affecting his attitude to the Bible that must at this stage be mentioned: the problem of its interpretation. Here we are not so much concerned with the ordinary aspect of this problem—this is, in a general way, the understanding of the application of the text from St. Paul quoted so often, and with such effect on Augustine, by St. Ambrose: "For the letter killeth, but the spirit quickeneth" (II *Cor.* III. 6)[13]—but rather with attempting to show that what Augustine (among other Christian authors) was doing was likewise part of a persisting and long-established tradition in the Platonist schools.

Philo Judaeus (*c.* 30 B.C.–A.D. 45) of Alexandria is credited with innovating the technique of applying Greek philosophy to the Hebrew Scriptures.[14] His method was that of the elaborate and extended commentary upon the text. His chief device in the application of Platonism to Scripture was allegory, an instrument used long before his time in the interpretation of Homer and Hesiod, and similarly used after his time by, for example, Porphyry. Porphyry also used the same method in his *Philosophy from Oracles*, which comprises the text of the oracles and his comments upon them.

By Augustine's time the commentary of this kind had to an extent supplanted the older vehicle of philosophical speculation, that was the dialogue. It is, therefore, a cause of no surprise that at an early stage of his career he should have thought of devoting his life to commenting upon the Scriptures, that in fact a great deal of his books are scriptural commentaries, and finally that the last twelve books of the *City of God* are in a sense the exposition of certain fundamental teachings of Revelation. Indeed, the frequency of the Scriptural commentary began to be an indication of Christian domination and the Christians' assumption of intellectual responsibility.

* * *

The inspiration for the idea of "city" of God has been sought in diverse places, from Plato's *Republic*[15] to the writings of the Donatist Tyconius.[16] It is true that there is discussion of political themes in the work—but one must add that this happens from time to time only. There is no suggestion that the city in question, the *ciuitas*, is to be thought of in terms of walls and houses, government and administration, army and police, internal policy or (in a political sense) external relations. There is no suggestion in fact of anything physical. Neither is there much help to be got from understanding Augustine's use of the term "city" in an "ideal"[17] or Platonic sense: as a model city in the truly existing world of intelligibles. Such a city, if the word is to have any meaning, must have the properties in a real sense that we observe in their shadowy participations and imitations here below.

A fresh and careful reading of the *City of God* will confirm the welcome tendency now manifesting itself of taking Augustine at his word. To the explicit testimony of the text from XI. 1, already quoted, we may add that of XIV. 1 where he with little less clarity indicates that the reference of his title is to the Bible, particularly the *Psalms*, and most particularly *Psalm* 86. 3: "Glorious things are said of thee, O city of God."

It is not merely that the word comes from the Scriptures: its application is no more precise than it is in Scripture. Augustine apparently saw no inconvenience in this; for the time and number of books devoted by him to his theme afforded him ample opportunity to be as precise as he chose. This is not to say that he allows himself to be inconsistent. His views as expressed in the *City of God* may conflict not only with the teaching adopted by the Church, for example, on the central matter of predestination, but also with his own views expressed elsewhere; but this does not affect the general consistency to be found within the work itself.

His statements, as a matter of fact, are clear enough as far as they go. He speaks, as we have seen, of the "city" of God, because Scripture has informed us of its existence. When he proceeds to describe what is meant, he usually calls it a "society" (*societas*): "these two societies of angels, diverse and contrary to one another" (XI. 34); "societies, as it were cities" (XII. 28); "two divisions of human society, which we can following our Scriptures rightly call cities" (XIV. 1); "city, that is society of the impious" (XIV. 9); "two divisions which mystically we call two cities, that is societies" (XV. 1); "the city of this world, which indeed is the society of impious angels and men" (XVIII.

18), and so on. Society, however, is not the only equivalent given for *ciuitas*; there are also "kind" (*genus*, XIV. 1; XV. 1), "house" (*domus*, XV. 19), "temple" (*templum, ibid.*): "whether it be called the house of God or the temple of God, or the city of God, it is the same"; family (*familia*, I. 35; cf. I. 29) and, by implication and in no more precise sense, "kingdom" (*regnum*, XXII. 30).[18]

Augustine defines the term *ciuitas* as being nothing other than a concordant multitude of men (*aliud non sit quam concors hominum multitudo*, I. 15), or again as being nothing other than a multitude of men bound together by some bond of association (*hominum multitudo aliquo societatis uinculo conligata*, XV. 8).

From these considerations one is led to the conclusion that the essential, if not sole, significance that Augustine wishes us to grasp from his use of the term "city" is quite simply the idea of association in itself. Other significations may be misleading, and the title has undoubtedly been the cause of much misunderstanding. His justification is that Scripture used the term. In view of the fact that the ancient city with its citadel, tutelary deity, and organized public worship was at least in part a religious entity,[19] the term had also a certain appositeness in the treatment of the subject of religion as it affected, for example, the Roman Empire.

The next point to determine is the nature of the bond that creates the association. Augustine is emphatic and crystal clear: "so that is the great difference, whereby each of the two cities of which we speak is distinguished; one a society namely of pious men, the

41

other of impious, each of them with the angels attached to them, in which has precedence in one the love of God, in the other the love of self" (XIV. 13). One is the society of those who freely serve the true God; the other is the society of those who freely refuse to do so. One is humble, the other proud; one clings to God, the other depends upon itself and does not cling to God. The two associations center on these two mutually exclusive focuses. The city of God is, reverting to Augustine's definition of the *ciuitas*, the multitude of men bound in association by the love of God.

Among the misunderstandings that have arisen from attaching undue importance to the term "city" is that Augustine is speaking, not of two cities—of those predestined to salvation and those predestined to damnation—but of three;[20] that is, the two mentioned, which may be described as the spiritual-heavenly city and the carnal-earthly city, with the addition of a third, the spiritual-earthly city. This is basically an attempt to provide for the apparent good of this world that yet does not and will not belong to the city of God. Must it be relegated to the damned city? With this problem we shall attempt to deal in due course. It must be said straightway, however, that any solution that implies a third city is in direct contradiction with the most explicit statement of Augustine: "nevertheless there exist no more than a certain two divisions of human society, which according to our Scriptures we may rightly call two cities" (*non tamen amplius quam duo quaedam genera humanae societatis existerent, quas ciuitates duas secundum scripturas nostras merito appellare possemus*, XIV. 1). Moreover, it is inconceivable that if Augustine had considered his theme in terms of three cities that he should never have said so, but always spoken of two.

We can now address ourselves to the question of what Augustine more fully means by the "city" of God.

The first thing to grasp, never to relinquish, is that the city of God exists already in heaven and, apart from certain pilgrim men who are on their way to it while they are on this earth, in heaven only. God's unchangeable will is its law. It is composed of the good angels and men who are saved. All these, and those who are yet to join them, were predestined to belong to this city.

On earth this city does not exist; but men, born outside it (and therefore in the other city) can become citizens of it and be on pilgrimage to it while they are here below: "the city of the saints is above (*superna*), although it brings forth citizens here, in whom it is on pilgrimage" (XV. 1). Christ is the founder and king of this city in its earthly connection. Entry to the city for men is through regeneration in Christ—by belief in His resurrection, "as long as the city of God, which is begotten of faith in Christ's resurrection, is on pilgrimage here" (XV. 18). Such of the Hebrews (who as a people prefigured the city of God, but who individually might or might not belong to it) as did belong to this city and such other men of what race soever (including the Erythraean or Cumaean Sibyl, XVIII. 23) as became its citizens, were enabled to do so through belief in Christ's mediation as revealed in prophecy or other divine means (XVIII. 47).

Such men as belong to the city of God are saved by grace: "nevertheless the omnipotent God, the most great and good creator of all natures, who helps and rewards wills that are good, but abandons and condemns those that are bad, while ordering both, was assuredly not without a means by which He might make up a fixed number of citizens, predestined in His wisdom, of His city, even from the condemned race of men" (*quo certum numerum ciuium in sua sapientia praedestinatum etiam ex damnato genere humano suae ciuitatis impleret, non meritis, sed gratia discernens*, XIV. 26). Without grace one cannot become, what one does not deserve to be, a citizen of this city (cf. XV. 2, 21).

It is to be remarked that Augustine here seems to imply, what elsewhere (XXII. 1) he states, that the human content of the city of God is intended to make up for the loss of the rebellious angels. In XXII. 1 he considers the possibility that more men may be saved than angels were lost.

The citizens of the heavenly city, preserving the right order in their love (XV. 22), clinging to God (*adhaerere Deo*, XII. 1), sacrificing to Him only (X. I), and living in the hope of God (XV. 21)—and not in earthly expectation—attain through salvation in Christ a state far superior to that which, if Adam had not sinned, would have been man's lot.[21] This gain is stressed by St. Paul in his Epistle to the Corinthians (I *Cor.* XV. 21f.): it represented a marvelous elevation of man's nature in Christ's resurrection (cf. XIII. 23). It is well to draw attention to this more optimistic aspect of the *City of God*, of which is often re-

44

membered only the pessimism that arises from pre-destination to damnation.

One question of great interest is whether the number of men in the city of God is great or small. Augustine tells us that its citizens are many (XVII. 2), but seems to imply, nevertheless, that they are few in comparison with the multitude of the impious (XVI. 21). This should mean that the majority of men are predestined to damnation. Moreover, we are informed that they who do not transfer their allegiance from the devil to Christ while they are alive are to be presumed to belong to the devil (*in parte diaboli computatur qui, dum esset in corpore, non est translatus in Christum,* XXI. 24).

The distinguishing mark of the city of God, insofar as it shares with the other city a common mortality, is the worship of the one true God. On this point there cannot but be variance between it and the other city, which is distinguished in refusing to worship the one true God, worshiping false gods instead.

The other city, known variously as the city of the Devil, the earthly (*terrena*) city, the city of this world (*huius saeculi*), and the enemy (*inimica*) city, exists here (XVIII. 1f; XX. 14; XXI. 1). It is composed of all those men and angels (XVIII. 18) who are predestined not to belong to the city of God. As we look around us we are looking at, for the most part, the human members of this city—but they are not distinguishable as such: any of them may before death join the city of God. When the end of the world comes and all men are dead, the cities of God and—

as it will then be most accurately described—of the Devil will no longer be indistinguishable.

Entry for men to this city is simply by birth and is inevitable; we are all born to it (XV. 1, 16), although we may pass out of it through Christ (XXI. 16). Our nature, indeed, is good, but it is vitiated by sin (XV. 2). This city has the Devil for its king (XVII. 20), draws its human membership from Adam's progeny (XV. 17, 21), and was founded by Cain, in whom it first began to appear (XV. 7, 17). The members of this city refuse through pride to cling to God (XIV. 13), turn away from the Creator (XIV. 5), and do evil in not observing the proper order in their use of even good created things—in which is their whole interest (IV. 21; XIV. 9; XV. 22). They are under the domination of the angels who forsook God (XVI. 17).

The distinguishing mark of this city is the worship of and sacrifice to idols and false gods (XVIII. 23, 54). It is deservedly damned in punishment (XV. 21), and that for eternity (XXI. 16).

One must be careful, of course, to distinguish between the city of the Devil, which is a mystical city of evil spirits and men who will not worship the true God, and the created nature which they use in common with the citizens of the city of God. This nature, as we have seen, has occasioned the suggestion that Augustine intends that there are three cities, not two. Before, however, we deal with the problem of this nature we should say something about Augustine's idea of what evil is.

It is essential to understand that for Augustine

evil is not something positive; it is rather a lack of something. It has, he says (XII. 6f.), no efficient cause: it may be said to have a deficient one. To use, for example, a created good for any end other than the worship of the Creator is evil: "The first evil will was indeed a declining from the work of God to its own works rather than any work" (XIV. 11). Again: "to forsake the Creator and live according to the created good, is not good" (XIV. 5). It can be seen, immediately, how Augustine, according to this doctrine, can refer to what is merely human, or merely humanly considered, as simply evil. This is the *absolute* canon by which all things are judged. If Augustine appears to relent from time to time and speak of goodness apart from this, he is speaking of what is only *relatively* good. This creates ambiguity and confusion of which the most notorious case is his inclusion of justice in the definition of the State in one instance and exclusion of it in another: but this we shall see later.

Many things have a limited or relative goodness: the flesh itself, female beauty, righteous victory, peace—indeed all created things insofar as they are created are good (XIV. 5f.; XV. 4, 22). Man unaided by any special revelation manifests this goodness in his ability to attain truth concerning the Creator and Providence, to practice virtues such as patriotism and justice, and to attain to friendship and good manners (XVIII. 41). Human virtue can even serve as an improving example for the citizens of the city of God (V. 18f.).

The reward, however, for this goodness is confined to this life: "they have received their reward" (XV. 3

47

[*Matt*. VI. 2]). As goodness it is inferior at its best even to the imperfect beginnings of the virtues of the citizens of the city of God (V. 18f.). Indeed a virtue that is without reference to God is but a seeming virtue and is, rather, *absolutely* vice. It lacks the true justice which exacts the recognition of the true God (XIX. 25). Merely human virtue ultimately involves the rejection of the true God, which is a disorder arising from pride (XIV. 9, 28; XV. 22; XIX. 24). The State, for example, considered from a merely human point of view, aims at dominance and worships what god or gods will help it thereto: this is a gross perversion of the proper order (XV. 7).

Nevertheless it still remains true that the created nature that is used in common by both the city of God and the city of the Devil is good in itself (XV. 22). This nature is not only physical; it also takes the forms of institutions and activities and enters into everything except the wills of evil men.

But since this nature exists here below—and therefore outside the city of God—it is natural that it should be confused with the city that exists here: the city of the Devil. At the same time Augustine more often than not avoids the term "city of the Devil" and speaks of the earthly (*terrena*) city, or the city of this world (*huius mundi*), formulas that—keeping to the actual words themselves—do not necessarily imply any suggestion of evil, or at worst suggest something less perfect and limited than what is described as heavenly (*coelestis*). Only the context will show whether Augustine intends by these terms the mystical city of the Devil or the relative goodness of created nature. When, for example, he says that the earthly city is not eternal (XV. 4, 17) he cannot mean the city of the Devil, which is eternal (XV. 1).

The things used in common, therefore, by the two great eternal and mystical cities are good, but limited and temporal. They do not constitute a third city, for the cities in question have to do with the wills of men and angels. These cities existed before earthly created nature and will exist when it is no more. In this earthly period, created nature is used by citizens of both cities who can share most things, with, however, the great exception of religion and worship: this is the great and significant divide.

It is evident that the two cities were predestined to be constituted as they are and that God's providence is operative in their realization. Attention must be called to Augustine's doctrine on these fundamental points.[22]

We have already seen the clear and somber text from XV. 1 where it is stated beyond doubt that one city is predestined to reign with God and the other to be condemned with the Devil for all eternity. Another text, for example, is no less clear: "What shall He give them whom He has predestined for life, who had given these things even to those whom He has predestined to death?" (XXII. 24).

In His providence God has forseen that those predestined to be damned will be useful for the saved and will afford a contrast between the two cities: the presence of evil makes the good more evident (XVII. 11; XXII. 1). Providence uses temporal disasters, such as wars, evil demons, and evil of every kind for its purposes (VII. 30, 33f.; X. 21). It broods over all, and through it those predestined to salvation are brought not to the perfection that was man's in Paradise, but the higher perfection of God's city (V. 1; XXII. 1).

Ultimately being a citizen of the city of God means salvation. Those who are still on earth are on the "way" to the fatherland; they are in the harbor whence they will pass to the fatherland itself. Here we recognize the persistence of Augustine's earlier ideas on man's destiny. Plain too is the continuance of his idea of the role of disaster and misfortune in the purposes of Providence. He had discerned this in the pattern of his own life as he had seen it at the time of his conversion. Now he discerned it in the life of mankind.

His picture of that life, presented from one point of view, is gloomy indeed. But we must, for all that, give some of it:

Book XXII. 22
... a darksome pool ... [of] heartaches, troubles, griefs, and fears; such insane joys in discord, strife, and war; such wrath and plots of enemies, deceivers, sycophants; such fraud and theft and robbery; such perfidy and pride, envy and ambition, homicide and murder, cruelty and savagery, lawlessness and lust; all the shameless passions of the impure—fornication and adultery, incest and unnatural sins, rape and countless other uncleannesses too nasty to be mentioned; the sins of religion—sacrilege and heresy, blasphemy and perjury; the iniquities against our neighbors—calumnies and cheating, lies and false witness, violence to persons and property; the injustices of the courts and the innumerable other miseries and maladies that fill the world, yet escape attention.

It is true that it is wicked men who do such things, but the source of all such sins is that radical canker in the mind and will that is innate in every son of Adam. . . .
. . . who can describe or even imagine all the later ills that befall mankind? Who can be free from fear or grief in a world of mourning and bereavement, of losses and legal penalties, of liars and deceivers, of the false imputations, violences and other wickednesses of our neighbors . . . of the tragedies of being robbed or reduced to slavery, of bonds and prison walls, of banishment and torture, of limbs cut off and eyes torn out, of bodies made to minister to an oppressor's lusts, and of all other no less dreadful possibilities.

And think of the dread we have of the countless accidents of nature, of the extremes of heat and cold, of winds and rains and floods, of thunder, lightning and winter storms, of earthquakes, landslides . . . of poisoned fruits and waters, of pestilential air . . . of the bites of wild animals.

The catalogue goes on and on, listing the miseries that befall man in the forests, the seas, journeys, accidents, plagues, floods, from the devils, diseases and their painful remedies, famine (which can lead a mother to devour even her child), frightening dreams, and hallucinations.

There is one thing that gives hope and deliverance in the end from all these miseries—the grace of Christ. Such comfort as human philosophy can afford must also ultimately be referred to Him whose gift philosophy is.

Finally comes the question of the role of the Church in the *City of God*.[23]

In a very general way Augustine identifies the Church with the city of God on pilgrimage here below. Thus he speaks of the "city of God, this is His Church" (XIII. 16); "the Church, which is the city of God" (XVI. 2); "that beloved city which is nothing other than the Church of Christ spread throughout the whole world" (XX. 11; cf. 8). The formula may vary from time to time; he may speak of the Christian religion (XVII. 4) rather than the Church; or he may allude to the "city of the great King" (XVII. 4); or to "Christ and His Church, that is the King and the city which He founded" (XVII. 15), or to "Christ and His Church as the King and Queen of the city" (XVII. 20)—but the identity is always there.

There were, however, serious reservations to this identity.

First, there were citizens of the city of God on the earth before the Church came into being. They became citizens by the grace of Christ, it is true; nevertheless they could not have belonged to the Church as a visible society. The Sibyl, for example, Augustine thought, must have been a citizen, since her verses had not only no tendency toward idolatry, but were all against false gods and their worshipers (XVIII. 23). The test he applies here is significant. The Hebrews, of course, although their aims were ostensibly purely temporal (IV. 33; V. 18; X. 14f.) and they were now the enemies of the Church (VI. 11; XVII. 17f.), had the approval and confirmation of miracles for their Law (X. 17), foreshadowed the city of God and gave it members (XVI. 3).

Second, the Gospel warnings of the cockle among

the good seed, the separation of the wheat from the chaff, and the mixed collection of fish in the net led Augustine to conclude that there were members of the Church visible who would not be found in the end to belong to the city of God. He was the more led to this conclusion from the observation that many were becoming Christians in his day for what seemed to be unworthy motives—sometimes merely for political protection or advancement. He believed that many would fall into this class (XVIII. 48f.; XX. 5,9).

Third, it was to be presumed that there were likewise men who did not belong to the Church and might seem not to belong to the city of God, who yet are destined for salvation and do in fact belong to that city.

In connection with this last point arises the question whether a man must now join the Church before death if he is to belong to the city of God. The testimony of the *City of God*, with which alone we are here concerned, is represented by the following text: "Let him, therefore, who wishes to escape eternal punishment, not only be baptized, but also justified in Christ and so truly pass from the devil to Christ" (XXI. 16). Or again: "but if any remain impenitent of heart until death, and are not converted from being enemies to being sons, does the Church then pray for them, that is, for the spirits of such dead people? (No) And why? Because he who has not passed over to Christ, while he was in the body, is already counted as belonging to the Devil" (*in parte iam diaboli computatur* XXI. 24). The presumption of their damnation does not seem to be absolute; but there equally seems little room for hope.

Augustine knew that a new era, the *tempora Christiana,* had already come. The persecutions, the martyrdoms, the hostilities of the Jews had not been in vain. Now those very Jews in their dispersion spread the Christian name. The fulfillment of prophecies and the independent conclusions of the secular philosophers, the confirmation of miracles, the political domination of Christianity, the evident decay of paganism and the overthrow of its idols—all gave assurance that few would remain outside Christianity. In Augustine's words, the whole world was running to Christ. In such a context one can understand that it would have seemed partly unnecessary and partly impolitic to dwell upon any other possibility of salvation than that afforded by the Christian religion.

The author of the *City of God* was, however, no millenarian. He believed that the world was declining and that Christ would gradually withdraw His flock from it (II. 18); he believed, moreover, that the world in his time was in its last age; but he insisted that we cannot know, and we should not speculate on, how long that age would endure (XXII. 30).

* * *

In the light of the previous analysis of the *City of God,* we might now address ourselves to the consideration of what validity there is in the popular and widespread notions that this work contains a "philosophy of history" or—a view that has spread more recently—a "theology of history."

54

A fair sample, and the likely source of some views on the former notion, is to be found in John Neville Figgis's *The Political Aspects of Saint Augustine's City of God* (London, 1921), in which the whole of the third chapter is devoted to the question whether or not Augustine puts forward a philosophy of history. He quotes the opinions of others to the effect that Augustine was a greater philosopher of history than Hegel or Vico, and was indeed "the true originator in the field of the philosophy of history." His general attitude is represented in the following passage:

No one who takes the Incarnation seriously can avoid some kind of philosophy of history. That event—if a fact —testifies at once to the importance of human life on earth, and shows its centre. Doubts of Christianity at this moment are largely due to the difficulty felt by many in making the events in Palestine the pivot of human history. The religion of the Incarnation cannot be mere theology —a system of notions developed from certain metaphysical propositions—nor can it be mere ethics, a code of laws on a theistic basis. It has to do with a life on earth in which Christians hold that in the fulness of time—*i.e.* at the due moment in history—the eternal reality at the heart of things became self-revealed and self-limited in a living earthly person. The issue of this was the fulfilment of the Jewish theocracy in the Christian Church. Augustine moreover approached Christianity emphatically by way of the Church. No one who did that could ignore the problems which it involved. Take a definite historical fact as your centre, take an actual visible society as the special sphere of God's operation, a society which has a past and must have a future on earth; and then you are compelled to some philosophy of history. You cannot, like a sheer Platonist—and Augustine shows leanings that way

—treat as of no account the whole development in time and space, as though this world were the dreams of the Absolute in a fit of absence of mind. . . . On the whole, his belief in the Church and his sense of immediate reality were too great. A man who does not give way to the temptation of a doctrinaire's system pure and simple, but has so much regard to the actual as S. Augustine, is bound to rest unsatisfied without some philosophy giving history a meaning [pp. 34f.].

Prescinding for the moment from the rather surprising description of theology as "a system of notions developed from certain metaphysical propositions," and ethics as "a code of laws on a theistic basis," we might ask ourselves what Figgis means by philosophy, which he applies to history? Philosophy has at various times meant various things, and its etymology, "love of wisdom," allows it to be very comprehensive; but on the whole its traditional meaning has been discursive reasoning on the subject matter of logic, physics, and ethics. While one must allow for development in the signification of terms and never bind oneself absolutely to rigidity in their use, one does well to conform to received practice in such matters, to use, in short, technical terms technically.

Does Figgis use the term in this way? Hardly! "Taking a definite historical fact as your centre and an actual visible society as the special sphere of God's operation" in effect means that you are dealing with history, theology perhaps, but not philosophy. Figgis betrays his position when he remarks that, as compared with Vico's *Nuova Scienzia*, Augustine's *City of God* is primarily concerned not with history but *apolo-*

getics: "Augustine is mainly concerned with the Church, Vico with the world" (p. 49). Or again: "It must be conceded that, to S. Augustine, history is the sphere of revelation" (p. 45). Figgis's whole discussion stresses the importance of the Fall, the doctrine of original sin (p. 41), the crises of Eden and Calvary (p. 36), the necessity to justify the Church (p. 37), and goes on to speak of the role of predestination (p. 45) and of world history as but an episode (in relation to Revelation, p. 39), and declares that "the paramount significance of the Church, viewed as the depository and dispenser of grace, is of the essence of this historical philosophy" (pp. 42f.). Philosophy seems hardly the proper word here.

Indeed, Figgis goes so far as to concede that Augustine did not set out to compose a philosophy of history. "His purpose was not to comprehend history, but to defend the Catholic Church" (p. 36). Or again: "Even if this be not a philosophy of history, strictly so called, it is at least a justification of the Church, historically conceived" (p. 37; cf. pp. 39, 42).

On the whole it is better to abandon the idea that Augustine in the *City of God* was attempting anything like a philosophy of history in any ordinary sense. Some indeed would hold that a philosophy of history is impossible: this is perhaps going too far, and it is possible that the phrase might legitimately be used of the discovery through reason of a pattern in the course of history. With this question we are not here concerned. Suffice it for us if from the method and contents of the work as we have seen them we conclude that at any rate the *City of God* gives no philosophy of history.

V. U. Padovani,[24] while insisting upon the views that there is not a philosophy of history to be found in the *City of God* and that a philosophy of history is in any case impossible, goes on to speak of Augustine as unifying history in the light of Revelation, not reason, and therefore as giving us, not a philosophy, but a theology of history.[25] This idea, first mentioned in 1861 by Cournot, has received notable currency in recent years, not, however, without some questioning even by those who advance it. Nevertheless to anyone who has read the *City of God* as a whole this idea is much nearer the truth about the work than that of a philosophy of history.

One should start, however, with having a clear idea of what is meant by theology. The *Shorter Oxford English Dictionary* describes it as "the study or science which treats of God, His nature and attributes, and His relations with man and the universe." This description would surely be accepted as being nearer the mark than Figgis's "a system of notions developed from certain metaphysical propositions." The essential point in the definition is that God is the object of theology.

Now the phrase "theology of history," properly construed, should mean that history was an object of theology, and so it is; but strictly speaking it can be such an object only inasmuch as it is history as looked at from God's point of view. To describe history as looked at from man's point of view as an object of theology robs the term of its proper meaning. On the other hand if one spoke of a theological interpretation of history, one's meaning would be perfectly clear, one would use words more accurately, and one would lose but little in foregoing the suggestiveness of the phrase "theology of history."

But let us see some of the statements of a distinguished recent commentator on this point, M. H. I. Marrou:

His [Augustine's] theology of history is a knowledge that has issued from the faith, and as such, *per speculum et in aenigmate,* partial, mixed with darkness, combining certitudes with lack of knowledge. One must search for the deep roots of this mystery of history.

The proper object of his theology, and I think of the theology of history, the historical object properly so called, is the economy of salvation.[26]

Marrou frankly recognizes that our despair, growing as this century proceeds, of ever understanding why and how civilizations rise and fall, or the significance of mortal effort in building them—in brief the problem of what he calls the Meaning of History—can not only not be relieved at all by purely rational speculation, but is only partly relieved by Revelation: a theology of history is a declaration of the *mystery* of history. This theology of history, moreover, concentrates upon the topic of salvation.

Revelation does indeed give a meaning to history and enlighten us on the problem of salvation. If one accepts that Revelation, one has at least a partial (from man's point of view) guide to the Meaning of History. And if one does not accept that Revelation, one at least has had a view offered that one has had to reject. One in short is dealing not with history, but with a Revelation's account of it; with a theological interpretation of history, not with theology, which tells us of God and history only insofar as God sees it.

A by-product of the interest in a theology of history is the impression occasionally conveyed that Augustine's *City of God* was the first major work to substitute the linear concept of man's destiny (according to which he is born, lives his life, dies, and lives eternally in either heaven or hell) for the cyclic, according to which his soul returns from earth to heaven and from heaven to earth in a succession of lives and bodily unions. It is emphatically true that one of the most important points considered in the *City of God* is this very question; and one of the most important and significant points on which Augustine rejects Platonism in every shape and form is this—and it is well to realize that the implication of his rejection is that he cannot be called a Platonist in any full sense— but one should not forget that Christianity did not wait for Augustine to propound what was essential to it. Moreover, it is assuming too much to suppose that the Platonic and cyclical view of man's destiny was commonly accepted by the ordinary Greeks and Romans, or the majority of them. The evidence of literature does not bear this out. Even of Virgil a recent writer has declared: "It is evident that for Virgil time is not cyclic, but linear. There is a meaning of history which defines itself at the moment in the foundation in the world of the Roman power."[27]

In brief the position adopted here is that the phrase "theology of history" is a phrase both unnecessary and misleading: it seems to offer a vague promise that it cannot redeem. The *City of God* most certainly gives a theological interpretation of history: this is enough for us.

Greek Philosophy

B

So much has been written on Platonism and Neoplatonism in Augustine over the last seventy-five years that the impression has been created that the Platonic influence on Augustine was not only extensive and important, but also in certain ways dominant.

While it is not necessary to describe[28] here the course of the various controversies on Platonism in Augustine since Boissier and Harnack in 1888 independently formulated the theory that at his conversion in 386 Augustine was a Platonist tainted with Christianity rather than a Christian tainted with Platonism, it is well to draw attention to the evil results of some of the excesses of this theory. In 1918, for example, when this theory was at its strength, one was presented with the following statements by Prosper Alfaric in his

L'évolution intellectuelle de saint Augustin: "he considered [the Christian tradition] only as a popular adaptation of Platonic wisdom" (Preface VIII); "morally as well as intellectually he was converted to Neoplatonism rather than the Gospel" (p. 399); "[Augustine's synthesis in 386] perceptibly modified the doctrine of the Master (Plotinus) in order to adapt it to the teachings of the Catholic faith. But its transformation of Catholicism was greater in order to bring it into accord with the philosophy of Plotinus, and it regarded [Catholicism] as but an inferior form of wisdom, good only for weak intelligences or beginners" (p. 515); and, "In him the Christian disappeared behind the disciple of Plotinus" (p. 527).

No serious scholar would now make such assertions. In the meantime, however, the general views of an earlier period on this matter have been adopted by nonspecialists and still are current and uncorrected. In 1930 Ernest Barker, in an introduction to a shortened version of the *City of God* that was later printed in the Everyman's Library and became, what it still is, the commonest introduction to Augustine's great work, wrote:

St. Augustine, as we have already had occasion to mention, was particularly influenced by Plato. He had read his dialogues in a Latin translation; he had read the Neo-Platonists' interpretations of their master; and he cites Plato again and again in the course of *The City of God*. St. Augustine carried the general thought of Plato into his own *general* thought; and through him Plato influenced the subsequent course of Western theology throughout the Middle Ages and down to the Reformation, which was indeed itself, in some of its aspects, a return to Plato and St. Augustine. "The appeal away from the illusion of things seen to the reality that belongs to God alone, the slight store set by him on institutions of time and place, in a word, the philosophic idealism that underlies and colours all Augustine's utterances on doctrinal and even practical questions and forms the real basis of his thought, is Platonic" [quoting Stewart, *Cambridge Modern History*, I. p. 579].

[Barker proceeds] "The history of Church doctrine in the West," Harnack has said, "is a much disguised struggle against Augustinianism." This is a deep saying, and we must attempt to gloss it. St. Augustine, we may say, imbued as he was with Platonic philosophy, always believed in the unchanging perfection of a God who always and everywhere acted by law. Against this clear and pure rigour of an unswerving general order it was natural that those should revolt who wanted a mysterious and emotional world, rich in insoluble riddles, and needing a mediatory and miraculous Church to give a mystical clue. Such a revolt was that of the Nominalists of the later Middle Ages. The trend of their thought turned them towards obscurantism. The individual became an ultimate mystery: God himself became an inscrutably omnipotent individual, acting indeterminately by His individual will. The Nominalists thus came to magnify the authority of the Church as the only escape from "the burden of the mystery"; they believed in *fides implicita*; and in them may be traced the tendency of the over-subtle intellect to pass through obscurantism to the acceptance of mere authority. It was against the Nominalists that Wyclif and Luther were both in revolt; and they both went back to St. Augustine for comfort and countenance. It would be too bold to say that St. Augustine inspired the Reformation. But it would perhaps be true to say that he took the sixteenth century back to the idea of a general order of the Universe, and back to a conception of righteousness based upon that idea" [Everyman's Library, *City of God*, pp. xvf., xxxvi].

It is suggested here that Augustine, "imbued as he was with Platonic philosophy, always believed in the unchanging perfection of a God who always and everywhere acted by law," and that, if he did not actually inspire the Reformation, he took the sixteenth century back to the idea of that law and away from a mysterious and emotional religion in a miraculous Church. Augustine's Platonism is said to be the basis of his position, against which there has been a disguised struggle in the West. It can be seen immediately that the question of Augustine's Platonism is of great importance and continuing interest.

Before we attempt to describe Augustine's Platonism as seen in the *City of God*, we must first remove from the picture given above by Barker, and retailed by others, certain grave misconceptions.

One cannot overlook that in these pronouncements of Barker he appears to depend without question on the authority of Stewart and, significantly, Harnack, for the core of his case. The nonspecialist can hardly do otherwise; the inconvenience is that he may generalize more than his source, and at any rate is accurate only to the extent that his source is accurate.

We shall see in the course of this chapter that Barker's main point that Augustine, "imbued with Platonic philosophy, always believed in the unchanging perfection of a God who always and everywhere acted by law," in contrast with those who accept mere authority, is seriously undermined by the fact that when Augustine quotes Plato in the *City of God,* which is infrequently, he quotes repeatedly the same text from the *Timaeus,* translated by Cicero, to the effect that Plato's God was *not* unchanging and deliberately contravened the established general order.

When Barker speaks of Augustine carrying the general thought of Plato into his own general thought, he is saying something both true and important. It is true, however, only in the sense that there was a philosophical stock in trade, common to all the schools, seen, for example, in the philosophical works of Cicero, and which was in a general way Platonic. In this sense Augustine—but among many others—might be called, as M. J. Maritain has called him,[29] a Christian Plato; for he did have this stock in trade and it does underlie his philosophical notions.

It is, however, quite wrong to say that Augustine was so affected by Platonic idealism as to set slight store on institutions of time and place: nothing could be further from the truth, as the content of almost every chapter of the *City of God* proves. Neither is it true to suggest that Augustine had little or no need for a mediatory and miraculous Church.[30] Such assertions can be made only by prescinding from his writings and generalizing from unjustified assumptions both about Platonism as it was known to Augustine and his attitude toward it.

It is of some interest to note that Reinhold Niebuhr, while also connecting Augustine with the Reformation, adopts a position directly opposed to that of Barker.[31] To Niebuhr, Augustine's outlook is Biblical and unsubordinated to Classical thought. St. Thomas Aquinas, in his view, was responsible for the subordination in question, and the Reformation was a revolt from St. Thomas in favor of the Biblical Augustine. Niebuhr speaks of Christian systems both before and after Augustine as being "inferior because they subordinate the biblico-dramatic conception of human selfhood too much to the rationalistic scheme, as was the case with medieval Christianity culminating in the thought of Thomas Aquinas . . ." (*Christian Realism and Political Problems*, 1954, p. 138). Or again, "It is in fact something of a mystery how the Christian insights into human nature and history, expressed by Augustine, could have been subordinated to classical thought with so little sense of conflict between them in the formulations of Thomas Aquinas" (*ibid.*, p. 127; cf. pp. 116, 124). Paul Tillich likewise sees in Thomism the dissolution of the Augustinian view.[32]

Before we proceed to examine the question of Platonism in the *City of God*, one at least of the most important evidences on the general question of Augustine's Platonism, we might take warning against the all too widespread notion, that Platonism, or Neoplatonism, in some way dominated him, from the opinions of two of our contemporary specialists. J. H. Waszink, for example, has come to the conclusion that Augustine absorbed some fundamental ideas from Platonism, but fewer than is generally thought; although he owed much to Neoplatonism, his method of treating problems from the point of view of the Bible prevents one from believing that his thought is greatly influenced by Neoplatonism.[33] M. F. Sciacca believes that the "Christian Platonism" of Augustine is a *correction* of rather than an inheritance from Plotinus; Augustine refused to accept Platonic dualism or Plotinus's teaching on emanation; he insists on the resurrection of the flesh and postulates the faith as the source of truth.[34]

* * *

In Platonism, Augustine saw the contribution of Greece to his own life, in the first instance, and to the Christian Era. Philosophy, its schools and disputations, was a Greek thing, or Roman only because Greece became a Roman province. The recognition, therefore, that Greece had its contribution to make to the new era and that that contribution is philosophy is explicit, not only in words, but in the emphasis given to the matter in the whole of Books VI to X inclusive. The matter is introduced as being of more importance than that considered in the first five books; the last book dealing with Greek philosophy, X, is the last of the negative books and is one of the most important books in the work; and the topic comes up again from time to time in the remainder of the work, especially toward the end.

It is well to make clear at once that when Augustine is speaking of Platonism he is usually speaking of all or any of the following: Plato, died 347 B.C.; Varro, died 27 B.C.; Apuleius (a fellow African from Madauros, where Augustine went to school), died after A.D.

161; but especially the Neoplatonists Plotinus, died A.D. 270, and Porphyry, died about 305. All of them, except Plato himself, lived in the Roman world, and Varro and Apuleius wrote in Latin. These two are discussed in Books VI-VII and VIII-IX respectively. Of all of them, Porphyry was both nearest in time and of greatest influence in the world of Augustine, and receives the closest attention in the *City of God*, especially in Book X. Plato and Plotinus receive only occasional consideration.

In addition to these sources of Platonic doctrine, we must also keep in mind the enormous body of Platonic thought transmitted by the divided inheritors of Plato, the Academics, the Neopythagoreans, and elements in other schools, much of which is to be found in Cicero, an author very well known to Augustine. Nor must we ever overlook the influence of persons of Augustine's acquaintance, especially when he was at Milan, who, such as Mallius Theodorus, were actively interested in Platonism.[35]

His knowledge of Platonism convinced Augustine at the time of his conversion that it had the rational answer to very many things, even if he subordinated it to the authority of Christ. His enthusiasm for it had abated by the time he was in the midst of the composition of the *City of God*. Nevertheless his admiration for it even then and to the end of the work and his life was sincere and generous. This arose, partly no doubt, from the recollection of the role Platonism played in his conversion, but perhaps even more because of its agreement with Christianity on many vital issues.

In the *City of God* he indicates precise points of agreement—as he understood it—between Christianity and the Platonists. They taught the existence of an incorporeal Creator, of Providence, the immortality of the soul, the honor of virtue, patriotism, true friendship, and good morals. Final happiness, moreover, they held to be attainable through participation of the soul in the Creator's unchangeable and incorporeal light (I. 36; VIII. I, 6; XI. 5; XVIII. 41). "They agree with us on many things, both the immortality of the soul, that the true God created the world, and on His providence, by which He rules what He created" (I. 36).

Augustine took some satisfaction in discovering in affirmations of the Platonists their belief in, in effect, the Christian God. Thus Varro, although at one stage he is said to have arrived no further than the idea of the world soul, at another is flattered with the possibility that what he called the world soul might rather be the Creator of the soul. The worship of this Creator he wanted to, but feared to, commend: it was certain that, while he had no belief in the Roman pantheon, he had confidence in the existence of some invisible force and all-powerful King (IV. 31; VII. 6f.; VIII. I).

Porphyry presented less difficulty in this matter: in his *Philosophy from Oracles* he accepted the Hebrew God as the true God (XIX. 23). He appeared to Augustine to go almost as far as the Christian Trinity: this is the burden of the very remarkable last nine chapters of Book X, which link up with the equally remarkable sections, describing his own personal experience, in Book VII of the *Confessions* (cc. 9ff.), where Augustine sees a correspondence between the Prologue to the Gospel of St. John ("in the beginning was the Word . . .") and the Neoplatonic hypostases.

In short it appeared to Augustine that the Platonists came very close indeed—closer than any other thinkers—to the Christian truth. Moreover they brought others to it, even when they themselves refused to follow. Who then was more worthy of earnest and sympathetic consideration?

There were two other reasons why, in Augustine's opinion, the Platonists should be heeded.

That philosophy was, like Revelation, also a gift of God is implicit in his idea of the relation of Faith to Reason.[36] Both derived from the same source, God, and even if their methods differed they both needed God's enlightenment. In general the mass of men were more helped by authority than by reason; but some there were whom reason greatly helped. Augustine was not alone amongst earlier Christians to invest philosophy with a quasi-revelatory character: Justin Martyr and Clement had preceded him in this.[37] To many, indeed, Hebrew Revelation and Greek philosophy seemed to describe the same things. Serious philosophy, therefore, such as was Platonism especially, should be heeded.

The other reason demands greater attention. So lively was Augustine's belief in Providence, arising from the pattern that he saw emerging from the vicissitudes of his own life, that he discovered a good result in everything. He gradually built up, elaborated, and constantly applied what one might call a theory of providential economy, which lies behind his views. The clearest statement of this theory is to be found in an early work *De Vtilitate Credendi* (On the Usefulness of Believing), A.D. 391, where he discusses three kinds of error, the third of which is beneficial: when, for example, a bad thing is (mis)understood by the reader in a right sense—as if one gathered (wrongly) from a phrase of Epicurus that he approved of chastity (10f.). Augustine was so enamored of the irony of such a situation that he declared that, if one considered the matter carefully, the whole fruit of reading was in this attained; moreover such an error did credit to the man who was deceived by it: *tertium est, cum ex alieno scripto intelligitur aliquid ueri, cum hoc ille qui scripsit non intellexerit. In quo genere non parum est utilitatis, imo si diligentius consideres, totius legendi fructus est integer, hic error non modo humanus est, sed saepe etiam homine dignissimus* (10). In the following paragraph he distinctly says that the reader may understand usefully *the contrary* of what the writer meant. Of the Platonists he explicitly says in the *De Trinitate* (IV. 23) that "although they were unaware of it, God acted through them, so that truth might everywhere resound."

It is difficult not to believe that this theory is related to his own experience with the Platonists at the time of his conversion: we have seen indeed the prominence he gave in the *De Beata Vita* to those who are set upon a height at the entrance to the harbor of salvation, who point out the way to safety to others, but who through pride do not possess the truth themselves. The clear implication of the idea is that Augustine at the time of his conversion misunderstood the Platonist position on presumably important points; that in doing so he was brought to the Church; and that later he discovered that the Platonists did not hold what he thought they held. The description of his conversion as it was affected by the Platonists and as it is set out in the *Confessions* (VII. 13ff.) makes it plain that at that time he either misunderstood or did not fully understand the Platonist position on, for example, the hypostases, the nature of Christ, and bodily immortality. Both the *Confessions*, however, and the *Contra Academicos* (II. 6) tell us that when he read the Scriptures, *after* having read the Platonists, he saw all things *for the first* time with real clarity.

In the light of these considerations one can see that Augustine's attitude toward Platonism seems favorable to the extent even that when he disagrees with it he does so not only without rancor but sees the possibility of good issuing from its very error.

This attitude should not, however, blind us to the true position. *Amicus Plato, sed magis amica ueritas* (Plato is a friend, but a greater friend is truth). Augustine's actual position is neatly summed up by himself when, speaking of the Platonists and apropos of the *City of God*, he says: "*With* whom or *against* whom we dispute" (*cum quibus uel contra quos agimus*, XXI. 7). Plato, Augustine thought, was greater than any of the gods, but for all that he was not as great as any believer in Christ (II. 7, 14f.). Christianity comes first, Platonism second. Near as it is, helpful as it is, great as are its common interests with Christianity against materialism, it has tenets that are at radical variance with Christianity. A Christian must ultimately be an anti-Platonist: *contra quos agimus.*

The Platonist who, in Augustine's view, came nearest to Christianity, but who actually became a most bitter enemy of Christianity, was Porphyry, with whom, therefore, Augustine in the *City of God* is particularly concerned.

Porphyry (232/3–*c.* A.D. 305) was born in Tyre, studied under Longinus at Athens, and in due course became the faithful follower and disciple of Plotinus, whose biography he wrote and whose works he edited. He was himself a prolific writer, regarding it as his mission to popularize the doctrine of his master. At the same time recent work on Porphyry has tended to portray him as a faithful disciple of Plotinus, it is true, but not an uncritical one. In fact the *City of God* itself shows Porphyry in the role of serious critic who is sometimes more affected by Middle Platonism in certain matters than by Plotinus. Moreover the traditional picture of Porphyry as one who was first uncritical, then under the influence of Plotinus became critical, and finally ended his life as an uncritical theurgist is being revised.[38] Be that as it may, by the time Augustine came to write the *City of God* "the Porphyrian philosophy," in the words of Courcelle, "was the reigning philosophy: only one philosophy remained, the Neoplatonic: the spiritual master was Porphyry."[39] We must not allow *our* notion of the relative philosophical merits of Plotinus and Porphyry to affect our judgment of how they impressed Augustine and his contemporaries.

74

Moreover, Porphyry received most particular attention from Christians. There is a story that Porphyry either was or was about to become a Christian, that he was badly treated by Christians, and that he reacted in violent hostility to Christianity. Certain it is that he wrote a series of fierce anti-Christian tracts of which the best known is his *Against the Christians*. This, however, was not the only work of his to engage the anxious replies of the Christians: his *Philosophy from Oracles*, which I have elsewhere[40] attempted to prove to be identical with the work referred to twice by Augustine (and by him only) as the *Return of the Soul*, was paid the compliment of extensive attention from several Christian apologists. Among these were Eusebius (died 339) in his *Praeparatio Euangelica*, the Africans Arnobius (*fl. c.* 300) and Lactantius (*fl. c.* 304–317), Theodoret (died *c.* 466), Claudianus Mamertus (died 474), Aeneas of Gaza (died *c.* 518), Philoponus (died *c.* 565), and Augustine in the *City of God*. The chief negative target of this latter book is the work or works which I shall refer to as the *Philosophy from Oracles*. It is as an answer to the *Philosophy from Oracles* that the *City of God* in the context of its own times can best be understood.

A reader unfamiliar with the religious and philosophical movements of the time of Augustine might at first blush have difficulty in seeing the relevance of a work bearing such a title as *Philosophy from Oracles* to a work commending Christianity and based on the Bible. Since, however, Augustine in the *City of God* explicitly speaks of the Scriptures as oracles, one discovers that in effect the *City of God* is matching the oracles of the Bible against the oracles to which Porphyry relates a philosophy with which, according to its preface, the *Philosophy from Oracles* is most concerned.

We have already touched upon this matter and need add here but a few instances to illustrate what Augustine had in mind to do. Isaac and Jacob, for example, are said separately to have received oracles (XVI. 36, 38); the Lord is said to have spoken in oracles (XVI. 21); and verses of the *Psalms* are described as oracles (*psalmorum oracula* XVII. 18). Among other instances the most important is Augustine's direct comparison of the oracles of Scripture with those of Porphyry in the *Philosophy from Oracles*:

This God of the Hebrews, whose greatness even Varro attests, gave a Law to his chosen people, a law written in Hebrew, not an obscure and little-known law, but one that has long been common knowledge among all people. And it is this Law that contains the words: "He that sacrificeth to gods shall be put to death, save only to the Lord." What point is there in seeking for further proof in His Law and Prophets concerning this matter? Indeed, there is no need to "seek" for evidences which are neither rare nor recondite; nor even to collect all those texts that are so many and so manifest, and to quote them here. They make it clearer than daylight that the supreme true God wishes sacrifice to be paid exclusively to Himself. Now, I offer but one statement. It is brief, majestic, terrifying, and true. It was spoken by that very God whom the most distinguished pagan scholars extol so splendidly. Hear it, fear it, heed it, lest death befall you if you disobey. He said: "He that sacrificeth to gods shall be put to death, save only to the Lord," and that, not because God needs anything, but simply because it is good for us to belong to God alone. For the Hebrews' Scripture sings: "I have said to the Lord, thou art my God, for thou hast no need of my goods" [*Ps.* 15.2, as quoted by Eusebius.]

We ourselves, who form His City, are His best and most worthy sacrifice. It is this Mystery we celebrate in our oblations, so familiar to the faithful, as I have explained already. And it was through the Hebrew Prophets themselves that the divine revelations were given that the symbolic sacrifices of the Jews would one day cease, and that thereafter all races would offer one sacrifice from sunrise to sunset, just as we see for ourselves this very day. But I have already quoted enough of such texts throughout this work (XIX. 23).

The contrast between the widely diffused (*omnibus iam gentibus diffamatam*) clear and frequent (*aperta et crebra*), summary, awesome, fearful, but true (*breuiter, granditer, minaciter, sed ueraciter dictum*) and divine dispensation of Scripture with another that is obscure and unknown (*obscuram et incognitam*), abstruse and rare (*abstrusa uel rara*) is perfectly clear. It is equally clear, since the oracles of the *Philosophy from Oracles* are explicitly being contrasted with Scripture throughout the whole of the chapter in question, that these oracles represent the dispensation that is obscure and unknown, abstruse and rare.

In passing it is convenient to observe that the central point of discussion in the *City of God*, as indicated here and as the work itself bears out, is the worship of the true God (as against the worship of false gods). This is more particularly expressed as sacrificing to Him: *sacrificans diis eradicabitur nisi Domino tantum* (*Exod.* 22.20) or, to use another scriptural phrase constantly employed in connection with the two cities: *adhaerere Deo* (*Ps.* 72.8). Between them, these two Scriptural phrases sum up the *City of God*.

Augustine maintained that the oracles that were the Scriptures were superior to those of the pagans in points that should appeal to pagans: their fulfillment, their confirmation by miracles, and their wholesale acceptance by multitudes. His ideas of divine economy and providence enabled him to admit that other oracles might help God's revelation of Himself, but they could not but be worsted by the gradual and ever clearer revelation set forth in Scripture. Porphyry himself, Augustine contended, was not wholly consistent in his attitude to the oracles he used. It was not clear, for example, if he was a willing or unwilling believer in these oracles; it was not clear whether he was credulous or critical in his attitude toward them; and since philosophy, according to its preface, was the main interest of his book, *Philosophy from Oracles*, the interpretation he chose to give to the oracles might be of more importance than the oracles themselves—and philosophy was in that context capable of a very wide understanding: in other words Porphyry's opinions might be of more importance than the declarations of the oracles.

What was clear was that Porphyry had accepted two important, however incomplete, facts from the oracles, which brought him nearer to Christianity than any other Platonist: the excellence of Christ and the fact that the God of the Hebrews was the true God.

To the oracles Christ was "most worthy," and "a man of most excellent wisdom." His soul was immortal in the heaven of the blessed. For them the God of the Hebrews was the one true God, the Generator, King, and Father. Worship of Him should be spiritual, in which we should offer the spiritual sacrifice of ourselves, adoring Him everywhere in chastity, justice, and the other virtues, making our life a prayer to Him, imitating Him and seeking Him in all things.

But the *Philosophy from Oracles* went even further than this. Here Porphyry is represented as believing that the knowledge of this God is a "gift"—something suggestive, in fact, of the Christian idea of Grace.

Where Porphyry and Augustine differed principally was precisely on the nature of Christ, the rejection or acceptance of Him as the universal way of salvation, of His incarnation, and above all His corporeal Resurrection. The description of the help that he got from the Platonists and his final rejection of them in favor of Christ as outlined in the *Confessions* (VII. 13ff.) and the highly charged "oracular" scene of his actual conversion (*Conf.* VIII. 29) invite one to think that the *Philosophy from Oracles* had a special significance for Augustine. This I have tried to develop in my *Porphyry's Philosophy from Oracles in Augustine* (cf. especially pp. 158–168).

To this great difference between Porphyry and Augustine we must now come. Far transcending in importance the abuse by Porphyry's oracles of the Christians (as against Christ) as polluted and impious and the deceived worshipers of demons was their refusal to accept Christ as more than a man—however elevated He might be after death—or the resurrection of His or any other body and its sharing in immortality with the soul. The painful and shameful nature of the death of Christ's body they took to be evident.

For Porphyry the union of a soul in heaven with a body was an abhorrence: his refrain is constantly found in the tenth book of the *City of God: omne corpus fugiendum* (all body must be fled). Porphyry's case was that happiness was possible for the soul *only* when it would never be joined to a body again. With the strongest commendation from Augustine for having done so, he had departed from the teaching of both Plato and Plotinus that the soul returned in a cycle from heaven to earth and even became joined to nonhuman bodies (X. 30; XIII. 19). Porphyry at least restricted return, if it happened, to human bodies. While this represented progress, in Augustine's view, toward the linear destiny believed in by Christians, it at the same time struck directly at the Christian doctrine of the resurrected body.

Augustine confronts Porphyry on this issue with the testimony of Plato (*Timaeus* 41):

Book XIII. 16
Some philosophers, against whose charges I am defending the City of God, that is to say, God's Church, seem to think it right to laugh at our doctrine that the separation of the soul and body is a punishment for the soul, whose beatitude, they think, will be perfect only when it returns to God simple, solitary, and naked, as it were, stripped of every shred of its body.

Now, if I could, in their own writings, find no refutation of this hypothesis, I would have to go to all the trouble of proving that it is not the body as such but only a corruptible body that is burdensome to the soul. That is why, as I quoted in a previous book, our Scripture says: "For the corruptible body is a load upon the soul." The additional word "corruptible" makes it clear that the soul is weighed down not by the body as such, but by the body such as it has become as a consequence of sin and its punishment. And even if "corruptible" had not been added, this text could have no other meaning.

The fact is, however, that Plato teaches, as plainly as can be, that the supreme God made the lesser gods with immortal bodies and promised to them the great boon of remaining forever in their own bodies, of which death would never deprive them. Why on earth, then, do these philosophers, for the sake of poking at the Christian faith, pretend not to know what they know full well, except that they would rather squabble and disagree among themselves than agree with us?

Just listen to the very words of Plato, as Cicero has translated them into Latin. Plato is supposing that the supreme God is addressing the gods whom he has made: "You who have sprung from seed of the gods, give ear. The works of which I am the parent and maker, these are imperishable as long as I will them to be, even though all else that has been put together can be taken apart. For, it can never be good even to think of putting asunder what reason has joined together. Since you have had a beginning, you cannot be immortal and indestructible; yet, by no means shall you ever suffer dissolution nor shall any decree of death destroy you, nor prevail over my determination which is a stronger pledge of your perpetuity than those bodies with which you were joined when you were brought into being." . . . (*Timaeus* 41)

This much . . . I think needed to be said in the face of those who are so proud of being, or of being called, Platonists that they are ashamed to be Christians. . . . Ever on the lookout for something to tilt at in Christian doctrine, they violently assail . . . belief in the immortality of the body, pretending to see a contradiction in our double desire for the happiness of the soul and its permanence in a body to which . . . it is bound by a chain of grief. They forget that their . . . master, Plato, has taught that the supreme God had granted to the lesser gods . . . the favor of never dying, in the sense of never being separated from the bodies which he had united to them.

Porphyry's position, as indicated by Augustine, and that it was affected by Christian teaching are to be seen from this other passage:

Book XIII. 19
I have already remarked . . . that, in Christian times, Porphyry became ashamed of this Platonic theory and proposed not only to free human souls from the bodies of beasts but so to liberate the souls of the wise from every bodily tie, that blessed souls, utterly disembodied, might remain forever with the Father. Not to be outdone by Christ, he denied the resurrection of incorruptible bodies, maintaining that souls will live forever not only without earthly bodies but without any bodies whatsoever.

The importance of the first of these texts in relation to Barker's assertions that Augustine, as opposed to St. Thomas, followed Plato in insisting upon an un-swerving general order—as against a "mysterious and emotional world, rich in insoluble riddles, and needing a mediatory and miraculous Church to give a mystical clue"—requires no stressing. Barker's case is based on an illusion. Moreover the frequency of Augustine's citation of Plato to which Barker refers, and which is very unremarkable indeed in itself, arises to a notable extent from Augustine's constant use of this passage from the *Timaeus* because he found it more useful in polemics on the Christian side than the Platonic.

Our main interest, however, in these passages at this point is to show how Augustine thinks of the rela-tions of Christianity and Platonism: the Platonist of immediate importance is Porphyry, and the point of immediate importance with him is the resurrection and immortality of a purified body. Porphyry had, Au-gustine says, under the influence of Christianity abandoned what was most characteristic of Platonism (*profecto abstulit quod esse Platonicum maxime*, X. 30), namely, the doctrine of metempsychosis. On the other hand he did not accept the idea of a glorified body being united to a soul eternally. Augustine agreed with him on the first of these two, but disagreed on the second.

The matter is brought a step further in XXII. 25ff., where there is lengthy discussion of this prob-lem. Here the argument deals with the Christian doctrine of the resurrected and glorified body being united to the soul for eternity. Augustine appeals to the instance of Christ's resurrection to indicate the fact; he appeals to the Platonists themselves to prove the possibility. From Plato he takes the point that mortal bodies can become immortal; from Porphyry, that souls should not return to earthly bodies; and from Varro, that bodies dispersed can be reassembled so as to be reunited to their souls: this supplies him with the authority of Platonism for the elements of the doctrine of Christian immortality.

This eclecticism may seem lighthearted; nevertheless it lent some support to the view that Platonism was fulfilled in Christianity. The fact that, in Augustine's view, Porphyry had been induced to advance from the doctrine of Plato and Plotinus of a cyclical destiny toward a linear one through the influence of Christianity (XIII. 19) pointed the way in which Platonism should go. Porphyry plays a very particular role in all this: on the one hand he clearly came nearest, in Augustine's view, to Christianity; on the other he in fact was leading the last-ditch battle of the Platonists against the Christians, and was their fiercest enemy. Augustine was disposed to think that Porphyry through pride was misled by the demons from worship of the true God to worship of false gods and that he was but looking for an excuse for his enmity when he refused to accept the doctrine of the resurrected and glorified body (*quaerentes, quid in doctrina Christiana reprehendant, exagitant aeternitatem corporum*, XIII. 16). This is, doubtless, wishful thinking; but this is what he says. Despite the general hostility of Greek philosophy toward polytheism; despite his own recognition of the Hebrew God; despite his reverence for Christ and his departure from his masters on the matter of metempsychosis; despite (in Augustine's view XIV. 5) the Platonist recognition of the goodness of the flesh in itself, and above all Plato's words in the *Timaeus*; despite all this and much more, Porphyry's pride delivered him over to the false gods and left him in an insincere disbelief in the cardinal Christian teaching on the immortality of soul and body. Here once again we come to the great division between the two cities: the love of self and the love of God; pride and humility; polytheism and monotheism. In short, Christianity was seen in this to be more philosophical, and carrying on the tradition of Greek philosophy; Platonism, on the other hand, was showing itself less philosophical.

It has been said that there is no important doctrine in Augustine that is not founded on an interpretation, erroneous or not, of the Bible.[41] A more conservative view,[42] which would deny that Platonism was a comparable influence on Augustine with the Bible, seems to have much more to commend it. It should be clear from the preceding considerations that, so far as the major work of the *City of God* is concerned, this latter view is an understatement.

At the end of his life Augustine, reviewing in his *Retractations* some of his earliest works when Platonism had its greatest influence upon him, expressed regret that he had spoken so favorably of his Platonist friend Mallius Theodorus (*Retr.* I. II), and went on to chide himself for using a Porphyrian-sounding expression (*penitus esse ista sensibilia fugienda*) in the *Soliloquia* (I. 14. 24). He feared that he might be understood to agree with Porphyry, who is explicitly named, on the impossibility of eternal bodies. Here he describes Porphyry quite simply as a false philosopher (*falsi philosophi*). These words were written about the time when he was finishing the *City of God*. They reflect accurately his view in the latter work of the *teaching* of Porphyry, the Platonist whom he honored with special attention.

For Augustine Platonism was, nevertheless, something great, valuable, and good, and Porphyry, the most learned of its recent exponents (*doctissimus philosophorum*, XIX. 22), shared in this admiration. The explanation of such rejection on the one hand and reverence on the other must lie at least partly in Augustine's perhaps nostalgic recollection of what Platonism meant to him just immediately before his conversion, which in fact it had helped. This carries with it the suggestion that the acceptance of Platonic *doctrine* by him was overshadowed by the *impression* that his encounter with the Platonic writings had made. Another instance of this may, perhaps, be seen in the case of his experience with Cicero's *Hortensius*, as described in the *Confessions* (III. 7ff.);[43] but it is a commonplace that books, if read at a critical juncture, can have an effect far transcending normal expectation.

In some such way must we understand that, although for Augustine the authority of the Scriptures was paramount and decisive, the Platonists both when they approached Christianity in their many and elevated doctrines, and even when they were in error and in opposition to a basic Christian teaching, received from him a sympathy and consideration that would justify us in believing that he saw in Christianity the fulfillment of Platonism, but not that Platonic doctrine entered into the positive teaching of the *City of God* in any remarkable way.

Rome

C

Ernest Barker, in his well-known introduction to the *City of God* in Everyman's Library, says that the "ultimate effect of *The City of God* is the elimination of the State" (p. xxii, 1947 ed.; cf. pp. xxxiv f.).[44] A less radical judgment on this aspect of the *City of God* is represented by the statement that the book combines "Plato's theory of Ideas and his political blueprints in the Republic."[45] These two views are erroneous, but they indicate the necessity to consider the *City of God* from this angle.

J. N. Figgis in his *Political Aspects of Saint Augustine's City of God* (Longmans, 1921) castigates several such unfounded notions—still, however, repeated in later books—such as that Augustine's purpose in his great work was to develop a theory of Church and State, as of the two swords; or to lay down an industrial and economic program for the Middle Ages, which was to be discarded in due course in the rise of capitalism; or to condemn the institution of the State in general, and the Roman Empire in particular, as evil. One can only suppose that such misunderstandings persist, partly because of the title of the work, which to those who have not read it may well suggest a book in some way or another in line with Plato's or Cicero's *Republic*, and partly because in the decay of interest in theology until very recent years more work was done on the political aspects of the *City of God*—at least in the English-speaking world—than on any other. Even so, neither the title nor the fact that there is some discussion of political matters, both directly and by implication, justifies the suggestion that in the work there is any formal and developed political philosophy or theory of an ideal State.

The English-speaking world has cherished other illusions too on the *City of God* and these have been shared equally in the British Commonwealth and in the United States.

Without taking account of those who would see in the British Empire the realization in some mystical way of God's city, one observes that more modest estimates of the role of the British Commonwealth in this connection have some currency. Take, for example, this passage which was published in 1960: "[Augustine] was also a great Roman, and not unmindful of the virtues of the Roman Empire and its place in the divine economy. Those who honour him can therefore well understand the hopes that many have built on the British Empire and Commonwealth.

As Empire is gradually transformed into Commonwealth, we may permit ourselves a guarded optimism that we are not watching the beginning of the 'decline and fall.' The Roman Empire was, as it were, a political Old Testament of the City of God. May not the British Commonwealth in its era fill for many the same role?" (Edgar H. Brookes, *The City of God and the Politics of Crisis*, Oxford University Press, pp. 9f.)

Americans, on the other hand, have also recently had their attention called to this matter in the following terms: "But perhaps our national temptation in this connection is a new form of the imperial ideal in which the civic idealism of the 'American dream' replaces the religious vision of brotherhood in God. If St. Augustine heard a modern American school or congregation singing with devout fervor:

> *O beautiful for patriot dream*
> *That sees beyond the years*
> *Thine alabaster cities gleam*
> *Undimmed by human tears!*

he would assume that these words referred to our true fatherland, the heavenly city which can be reached only after the sin and sorrow of this earthly pilgrimage are ended. And we should have to tell him that for many of those present there was no truer heaven than the future United States of America." (Edward R. Hardy, Jr., "The City of God," p. 258, in Roy W. Battenhouse, *A Companion to the Study of St. Augustine*, Oxford University Press, 1955.)

The two instances given refer to modern, and

rather secular, developments of earlier apocalyptic interpretations of the *City of God*. Religious refugees from Europe, for example, in the sixteenth century partly hoped to *realize* the city of God on earth—a theocratic State of Massachusetts, for instance—and partly, yielding to circumstances, recognized that while they might constitute themselves God's city, there was present all around them the city of the world from which they must expect persecution. These ideas characterized especially the Puritans of New England, who have influenced in this way the general quality of Protestantism in America. This has been marked, as Richard Niebuhr has said,[46] not as in Europe by preoccupation with justification by faith, but rather by the conception of the Kingdom of God. Niebuhr has observed the declension in that conception from the spiritual notion of God's sovereignty to the more recent material one of a kingdom on earth; earlier ideas of building Sion on the Mississippi have faded before vaguer notions of the American dream. But all the time the idea of the city and the kingdom upon earth have been at work.[47]

The foregoing and other considerations—such as the question as to whether or not Augustine includes justice in the definition of the State—make it imperative for us to examine the *City of God* in its relation to things political and especially the Empire of Rome.

* * *

But first it is important to realize how Roman was the attitude of Augustine and how Rome was the center of his human interest. There has been so much discussion of Augustine the Platonist that Augustine the Romanist has been neglected, and it has been possible for such as Harnack to attribute to him the view, surely a priori improbable, that the independent state was the kingdom of the Devil.[48]

One must recall very briefly that Augustine grew up in North Africa within a family that supported Rome, was educated according to Roman methods, and embarked on the characteristically Roman career of Rhetor—which often led to high administrative posts within the Empire. Rhetoric marked the very soul of Rome: Rome was pragmatic, eclectic, less interested in metaphysics and eschatology than in ethics and how to achieve happiness. Even the most spiritual of the Romans recoiled from the unambiguous championing of idealism. Virgil for all his wistful mysticism has left us with many doubts on his ultimate philosophical persuasions. Cicero is hardly more clear. And even these two are less typical than, say, Horace with his *aurea mediocritas*, his golden mean.

Great as certainly was the influence of reading something of the Neoplatonists in translation, or even with less ease in Greek, the influence of Roman rhetoric on his mind was all-pervading and is to be seen on almost every paragraph that he wrote, and on many an argument that he used. He is by no means always innocent of the unrealities, exaggerations, and frigidities that characterized the profession he had espoused and practiced. "If one were asked," he remarks in the *City of God* (XXI. 14), "either to endure death or childhood again, who would not be aghast and choose to die?" Unhappy as his experience of childhood must have been, one would hesitate to conclude that rhetorical exaggeration and unreality had no part in such a terrible declaration. We have already taken note of a remarkable employment of eclecticism in an argument of the gravest import and seriousness: "[the Platonists] agree with us that even blessed souls will return to bodies, as Plato says, but will nevertheless not return to any evils, as Porphyry says, and take this also from Varro, that they will return to the same bodies, in which they were formerly, then their whole difficulty about the resurrection of the flesh for eternity will be solved" (XXII. 28).

With regard to this very question of the eternity of the flesh, the Romans, although they might reject it for other reasons, would have had less difficulty than a true follower of Plato, for whom only non-material things could have existence. There was, indeed, a strong materialistic bias in the philosophies that most affected the Romans that would have helped in this. Moreover the Roman, when he was not a materialist, was a skeptic. Basically he was a pragmatist, and his attitude toward the doctrine of bodily immortality would be determined less by fine philosophical reasoning than by more practical considerations. Augustine, as a matter of fact, had been a materialist Manichee for the whole of his twenties and had subsequently professed himself to be a skeptic,[49] a follower of the New Academy. It is too much to assume that his acquaintance with the Neoplatonists obliterated the attitudes of earlier and formative years; his eclecticism from Plato, Porphyry, and Varro on the question of bodily immortality is a significant reminder of how thoroughly Roman Augustine continued to be.

The fact that Augustine does not inform the reader from time to time throughout the *City of God* that he is considering his problem not only from the personal point of view but also from the point of view of Rome should not lead us to believe that this is not the case. One of the characteristic traits of Augustine is to assume that the reader will not need to be informed of what, to Augustine, was obvious.[50]

A simple and clear instance of this can be seen in his lack of reference to the source books used in the *City of God*.[51] There are hundreds of allusions to Varro's *Antiquitates*, but the title is given only once; there are frequent references to Apuleius's *De Deo Socratis*, but the title is given only once; there are over seventy references to the *Aeneid*, but the title is given only once; and there are over a dozen references to Sallust's *Catilina*, but the title is not given at all. The works of Claudian, Ennius, Lactantius, Livy, Lucan, and Persius are used, but again no title is given. Sometimes he uses a descriptive title, which would not have misled his contemporaries, but may not be even noticed or may be misunderstood by us: a crucial instance of this may occur in the tenth book in connection with a work of Porphyry's of the greatest importance for the argument of the *City of God*.

So it was with Rome. For his contemporaries, whose outlook on the world was bounded by the Roman Empire and its institutions, it was unnecessary, and might have been tedious, to have constant reference to what for them was the *praesuppositum* of the argument. Rome was the background and the foreground and the whole context of the work. Even when philosophy leads him to Greece and theology to the Hebrews, his purpose is that Rome should be fulfilled in both.

Nevertheless Augustine does make the point most explicitly. We have already seen Chapter XXII of Book XIX, which gives in dramatic and sharpest outline the focuses of the whole work. There the question is asked: "Who is that God or how is He proved worthy, whom the Romans should obey, so that apart from Him they should worship none of the gods with sacrifices?" The *City of God* is basically concerned with that question, and it is asked in the interest of, not the Greeks or the Jews or any other people, but the Romans. The answer to the question is, as we have seen, that the testimony of the Hebrews, of the Greeks (represented by Porphyry), and of the Romans themselves (represented by Varro) was that the Christian God was that God.

Once again one should not fail to notice in the text just referred to the spirit of electicism and reverence for authority. It might be said with some justice that Augustine was aware that there might be difficulty in getting Porphyry and Varro to accept his interpretation of their positions in favor of Christianity—and he did not conceal this. Augustine's fondness for a synthesis with firm outline, however, is more evident here than any purely philosophical argument. Some might see in this a basic Roman skepticism allied with a fondness for action, a preference for will as against intelligence, for authority as against reason. It is not surprising, indeed, that, although Platonism was received in Rome, the Bible and the Christian Church became the instruments for her of a new glory and a longer life. That this should be so was the positive purpose of the *City of God*.

It is essential that we should attempt to clarify Augustine's attitude on the question as to whether or not justice should be included in the definition of a State. Some are of the opinion that in his view a State was based on injustice—which of course would make him pessimistic about, if not actually hostile to it.

A *res publica*, he says (XIX. 21), according to the definition of Scipio as given in Cicero's *De Re Publica*, is the *res populi*. A populus, or people, Scipio defined as an association of many persons bound together by agreement on right and a common interest (*utilitas*). Scipio explains that by agreement on right is implied for him that a State cannot function without justice. Therefore where there is no true justice (*uera iustitia*) there can be no State. Justice is defined as the virtue that gives to each his own. How can man be just, then, if he takes himself from God and gives himself over to wicked spirits? For justice demands that men and their sacrifices should be given over to the true God and to Him alone. The Romans failed in this: therefore, if justice is to be included in the definition of a State, the Romans never had a State. "True justice does not exist except in that State whose Founder and Ruler is Christ" (II. 21), that is, the city of God.

"Pause," urges Norman Baynes in *The Political Ideas of St. Augustine's De Civitate Dei* (ed. 1949, pp. 7f.), "for a moment and consider the effect of this discussion upon Augustine's view of the character of a State. There was in the early Church a strong tradition that the maintenance of justice was an essential part of the purpose of the State: St. Paul had urged obedience to the State upon the ground that the State rewards the good and punishes the evil. Clement of Alexandria had defined a king as one who rules according to law, while Ambrose, Augustine's own master, had contended that justice and beneficence are the essential virtues for any community; justice—*aequitas*—is the strength of the State and injustice spells its dissolution. There have been attempts made to show that Augustine does not really mean to exclude justice from the definition of the State. . . . But as Mr. Christopher Dawson has written (A *Monument to St. Augustine*, 1930, p. 63): 'the actual tendency of the passage (*remota itaque* . . .) appears to be quite the contrary. . . .' There cannot be much doubt that Augustine meant what he said. 'If he did, I cannot but feel,' says Mr. Carlyle (A. J. Carlyle, *History of Mediaeval Political Theory in the West*, 1903), 'that it was a deplorable error for a great Christian teacher.' "

One is reluctant to believe that Augustine was actually in conflict with St. Paul and the strong Christian tradition. Appeals to the authority, even of Mr. Christopher Dawson, are not decisive. Since this is an important point, let us look at the context and see what Augustine did say and mean:

Book IV. 3
Hence, if the true God is adored, and if He is given the service of true sacrifice and of an upright life, then

97

it is beneficial for good men to extend their empire far
and wide and to rule for a long time. This is beneficial,
not so much for themselves as for their subjects. . . . But
the rule of wicked men brings greater harm to themselves,
since they ruin their own souls by the greater ease with
which they can do wrong.

As for their subjects, only their own villainy can harm
them. . . . Thus, a good man, though a slave, is free; but
a wicked man, though a king, is a slave. For he serves,
not one man alone, but, what is worse, as many masters
as he has vices. For, it is in reference to vice that the
Holy Scripture says: "For by whom a man is overcome,
of the same also he is the slave." (II *Peter* 2.19)

In the absence, therefore, of justice, what is sovereignty but organized brigandage? (*remota itaque iustitia,
quid sunt regna nisi magna latrocinia?*)

It is abundantly clear from the *itaque* (omitted,
perhaps unconsciously but significantly, by Baynes, p.
7) that the *iustitia* in question is the justice referred
to in II *Peter* 2.19–21.

For by whom a man is overcome, of the same also
he is the slave. For if, flying from the pollutions of the
world, through the knowledge of our Lord and Saviour
Jesus Christ, they be again entangled in them and overcome: their latter state is become unto them worse than
the former. For it had been better for them not to have
known the way of *justice* than, after they have known it,
to turn back from that holy commandment which was
delivered to them [vv. 19–21, Douay version].

Whether *remota iustitia* is taken as implying that
there *is* no justice in kingdoms or more probably as a

98

hypothesis (*if* there be no justice), the justice in question is "the holy commandment," "the knowledge of our Lord and Saviour Jesus Christ," and "doing worship and service to the true God in true rites and good morals." Augustine has gone to the microcosm to discover the truth about a macrocosm: has posited a good man and an evil man as exemplars from which to come to conclusions about "kingdoms, provinces, nations, or such." In other words, we are back again to the heavenly and the earthly man, the city of God and the city of this world: "Well then, even as we have done with these two men, so let us do with two families, two nations, or two kingdoms" (IV. 3, translation by Healey).

In brief, the text *remota itaque iustitia . . .* is speaking of justice not in any historical or ordinary sense but in an absolute and theological one. The situation is exactly as is described in the passage already quoted from XIX. 21 or as indicated in XIX. 24: "For in general the city of the unholy, which God does not direct obedient to Himself, so that it does not offer sacrifice but to Him alone, is without the truth of justice (*caret iustitiae ueritate*)." Augustine is careful to indicate that he is speaking of *true* justice in all these instances—presumably in contrast to some other justice that is imperfect.

Before we pass on to consider this other justice, we should attend carefully to Augustine's attitude when he faces himself with the inevitable theological conclusion that since the true God was not worshiped by Rome, if true justice—involving such worship—were to be included in the definition of a State, Rome could not be described as a State. Augustine took no satisfaction in such a conclusion, but rather than accept it for Rome was willing to go to the extent of defining a State without reference to justice at all. He proposed, therefore, to define a people as an association of many rational persons bound together by a concordant and common interest in things it loves (XIX. 24). According to this Rome, *pro suo modo quodam*, in her own way, was a State.

It is plain that in II. 21 also, Augustine is driven to this extreme position because of the main thesis of the *City of God*, which centers on the true or ultimate justice that worship and sacrifice be offered to the true God alone.

Book II. 21

. . . I shall endeavor to show that that ancient creation was never a true republic (*res publica*), because in it *true* justice was never practiced. I shall base my position on Cicero's own definitions, in the light of which he briefly determined, through the mouth of Scipio, what was a republic and what was a people. There are many confirmatory opinions expressed in that discussion both by himself and by the interlocutors he introduced.

However, according to some definitions that are nearer the truth, is was a commonwealth of a sort, and it was better governed by the earlier Romans than by those who came later. But, *true* justice (*uera iustitia*) is not to be found save in that commonwealth, if we may so call it, whose Founder and Ruler is Jesus Christ—for, no one can deny that this is the weal of the people. This name, with its varied meanings, is perhaps not quite in tune with our language, but this at least is certain: *True* justice reigns in that state of which Holy Scripture says: "Glorious things are said of thee, O City of God."

It could not be clearer that the *remota itaque iustitia* that has caused so much difficulty and shocked so many commentators is properly glossed by the phrase above: *uera autem iustitia non est nisi in ea republica, cuius conditor rectorque Christus est.* He is all the time speaking of justice that is *uera.* In the passage just quoted he has used the adjective as many as three times.

But just as we saw that Augustine provided for a *relative* as well as an *absolute* good, so we may presume that beside the *uera iustitia,* so important for the *City of God,* he would be willing to concede the existence of a *iustitia* that was not *uera;* a justice that, if judged absolutely and with reference to our duty to the true God, was not justice at all; but if judged by less absolute standards, could nevertheless be considered in its own way some kind of justice.

It will be seen how important it is to keep in mind the distinction between what is absolute and what is relative in relation to arguments involving theological positions in Augustine. His tenaciousness to an absolute view in this matter of justice is an indication at once of his willingness to adopt a position so extreme as to be misleading, and of the importance he attached to the Romans giving the true God the worship that was His due.

Augustine's attitude to Rome itself is, as one might expect, also twofold: theological and historical; she was *absolutely* evil; but *relatively* had a limited goodness.

As the head of the earthly, as opposed to the heavenly, city (*caput terrenae ciuitatis*, XV. 5) she stood condemned. In particular her submission to impure demons and false gods (XVI. 17; XIX. 21) marked her corruption and gave her the mystical character by which she is contrasted with the other mystical city. These demons led her astray into evil rites and practices (II. 6), and in particular debauched her people by the unclean plays of the theater (I. 31f.), in connection with which, therefore, Augustine seems to have almost an obsession. Finally they were responsible for excesses in war—for Mars, Bellona, and Victoria had to have their full measure of cult and honor (V. 17). The demons, in short, caused that pride, vainglory, and lust to dominate (XV. 7) which were irreconcilable with the heavenly city and the worship of the one true God.

It is difficult for us nowadays to think of these false gods and demons with the same sense of immediacy with which Augustine and his contemporaries thought about them. Yet we must do so, if we are at all to grasp the central argument of the *City of God*. These demons could manifest themselves physically—or at least create the illusion of their physical presence—as they had done in Campania, where they had been seen "to fight a set battle amongst themselves. At first there were strange and terrible noises heard; and afterwards it was affirmed by many, that for certain days together one might see two armies in continual fight one against the other. And after the fight had ceased, they found the ground all trampled up as with steps of men and horses that had been made in the battle" (II. 25, translation by Healey). Whatever credence Augustine gave to this story of the physical intervention of the demons, he had no doubt whatever about their spiritual interference in the lives of men and States.

It is necessary to know what kind of beings these demons were believed by Augustine to be. They were in fact the fallen angels (VIII. 22), led by Satan, who, of course, although the leader of his city, is not an enemy on equality with God. These demons or gods (for they can also be so called) are good by nature but evil by will (XII. 1):

Book IV. 1

. . . the false gods . . . were unclean spirits, malignant and lying demons. The truth of this is clear from the fact that these demons go so far as to take delight in their own villainies, to the extent of wanting them exhibited, either as facts or as fictions, in the festivals celebrated in their honor . . . as long as these villainies are exhibited for imitation under divine sanction, so to speak, it is impossible to restrain weak humans from actually reproducing in their own lives the abominable acts committed by the gods.

Book VIII. 22

These demons are spirits ever itching to injure, completely removed from righteousness, puffed up with pride, livid with jealousy, adroit in artifice. They may inhabit the air, but that is because they were cast down from the sublimity of high heaven, condemned to this place as to a prison in punishment of their irremediable transgression.

The demons had various important fields of activity: as against men of any kind they were far superior in prophecy, the use of dreams, magic, and miracles (cf. VIII. 16; IX. 22). Their knowledge of the future was similar to that of the good angels; but, unlike the good angels, they sometimes went wrong (IX. 22). The simplest man, however, could excel them by becoming a citizen of the city of God.

The aim of the demons was to attract worship and sacrifice away from the true God to themselves—to be treated as gods (VIII. 22; cf. IX. 7). Their powers were so great that they succeeded in this. The Platonists, however, for example, seemed not to be deceived, but in order not to cause offense gave them some of the honors due to God. Christians, on the other hand, are allowed by Providence to be subjected to compulsion to sacrifice to them; and when they refuse they win the crown of martyrdom (X. 21).

Augustine protests in XIX. 21 that no one who had read what he had so far written could doubt, unless he were stupid or merely contentious, that the Romans worshiped the evil and impure demons. He was, therefore, attacking, not Rome (as Baynes says, *op. cit.*, p. 16) but the service of the gods that she worshiped and to whom she sacrificed. He could not be more explicit than he has been that the *City of God* is concerned with religion (XI. 5), that his target is the cult of the false gods, and that the occasion of his argument is the prohibition of that cult in Christian times (I. 14; II. 2; VI. 1; X. 18, 32; XI. 1; XIV. 28; XIX, 17; cf. *Retractations* II. 43).

It has been well remarked by Ladner that for the

pagans the cult of the (false) gods was the central focus of the city. Kamlah has suggested that the fundamental idea of the *City of God* is the destruction of the gods, a view in which he is strongly supported by Ziegler. Everything that we have written most strongly confirms and amplifies this.[52]

Speaking of the two cities, Augustine says: "Both cities observe a peace in such things as are pertinent to this mortal life . . . [but] the two hierarchies could not be combined in one religion, but must needs dissent herein" (XIX. 17). The Sibyl, even though she preceded Christ and was not a Hebrew, seemed to Augustine to have been a citizen of the city of God *because she spoke against false gods* (XVIII. 23). Insofar as Rome or any Roman sacrificed to false gods they were absolutely condemned by Augustine.

On Rome's goodness, however limited, it will be best to listen to Augustine himself:

Book V. 12

. . . the earliest and most primitive Romans, like all other peoples with the single exception of the Hebrews, worshiped false gods and offered sacrifices, not to God, but to demons. Yet . . . they were "avid for praise, liberal with money, pursuers of high glory and hard-won wealth." Glory was their most ardent love. They lived for honor, and for it they did not hesitate to die. This single measureless ambition crushed their lesser greeds. It was their glory to conquer and control others, and a dishonor for their fatherland not to be free. . . . "The city grew at an incredible rate, because of their passionate greed for glory." Thus, passionate greed for praise and glory worked many wonders worthy, according to human standards, of praise and honor. . . . It is well . . . to go to Cato for an opinion on the state of the city. . . . "Do not think," he says, "that our fathers made our city great by arms. Had this been the case, we would have a far finer city than we have. . . . They had other means to make them great, which we lack: industry at home and justice in their rule abroad, a spirit of freedom in political discussion unstained by wickedness or lust. . . . the administration continued to be directed by a small group of relatively good men, through whose foresight the evils of the times were tempered and made sufficiently tolerable for the general welfare to continue to increase. This is Sallust's explanation (*Cat.* 7, 52).

Book V. 15

After all, the pagans subordinated their private property to the common welfare, that is, to the republic and the public treasury. They resisted the temptation to avarice. They gave their counsel freely in the councils of the state. They indulged in neither public crime nor private passion. They thought they were on the right road when they strove, by all these means, for honors, rule, and glory. Honor has come to them from almost all peoples. The rule of their laws has been imposed on many peoples. And in our day, in literature and in history, glory has been given them by almost everyone. They have no right to complain of the justice of the true and supreme God. "They have received their reward."

According to Augustine's thesis, ultimate reward is reserved for the citizens of the city of God, as ultimate punishment is for the citizens of the city of the Devil. There is no harsh judgment, then, in refusing to the pagan Romans, citizens of the earthly city, the greater reward. On the contrary there is a positive recognition here of a virtue that is relative, crowned with a corresponding reward.[53]

If Brutus, Torquatus, Furius Camillus, Scaevola, Curtius, the Decii, Marcus Pulvillus, Regulus, L. Valerius, Q. Cincinnatus, and Fabricius—all of whose names are recited with admiration, if not also pride, by Augustine (V. 18)—are not supposed by Augustine to belong, as did the Sibyl, to the city of God, it is because they did worship idols. Nevertheless Augustine commends their virtues, which were considerable; their love of glory and freedom, their love of honor and honesty, their willingness to make sacrifices for their principles, and their respect for law.

He goes further: God, Augustine says, in His providence gave the Romans help in erecting their city and Empire and let them have sovereignty when and for as long as it was His pleasure (V. 19, 21). God in fact resolved to erect Rome in the West to be superior to the monarchies of the East in greatness and dignity (IV. 15). As it happened, it was Rome's opposition to evil that brought about so much of Rome's conquest, so that through wars that were honest, upright, and just Rome was providentially compelled to grow.

The fulfillment of the mission of pagan Rome, however, was to be seen in its providing what should be an irresistible stimulus to Christians to be more virtuous for an immeasurably greater reward:

Book V. 16
It was, then, not only to reward the Roman heroes with human glory that the Roman Empire spread. It

had a purpose for the citizens of the Eternal City during their pilgrimage on earth. Meditating long and seriously on those great examples, they could understand what love of their Heavenly Fatherland should be inspired by everlasting life, since a fatherland on earth has been so much loved by citizens inspired by human glory.

Even more: Augustine declared that the Romans were found worthy by God to enslave the Hebrews, until recently the very shadow of the city of God on earth, because they had misused their advantages (V. 18).

Augustine was implacably hostile to Rome's gods; it is impossible to believe that, theology apart, he was other than proud of and favorable to Rome.[54]

The measure of his favor for Rome is to be seen in the future destiny he foresaw for her: she was to be at once fulfilled in Christianity and to help, by her own unity and extent, its spread—Rome's Empire was an instrument in man's salvation.

Throughout the *City of God* the rigor of the doctrine there set forth on predestination is tempered, partly by consideration of the greater destiny available to man than was available before the Fall, and partly by the optimism engendered by the spectacle of the multitudes—however unworthy and unlikely to persevere some individuals were—running to Christ.

The question naturally arises if Augustine had some vision of a Roman theocratic State or some close union between the Church and the Roman Empire. Although the idea of the union of Church and State is natural to the ancient city, and although later ages attributed such a vision to the *City of God*, and although the relic of such a reality still persists in Established Churches, Augustine did not in fact treat of the problem directly or clearly.

It appears, however, from what seems the somber teaching that the majority of mankind is damned that, if the Church is not to fail in her mission to save her members, she will not have dominated any one universal State, or a majority of populations organized in States from the beginning to the end of time. This, however, does not preclude the possibility that a State, and in particular the Roman Empire, might have some special union with the Church. Here again this would not preclude the possibility that the Roman Empire for a time might have such a union, and later might not: Augustine, as we have seen, was no millenarian.

We must further observe that a union might mean anything from a strict theocracy, which, according to the *Shorter Oxford English Dictionary*, is "a form of government in which God is recognized as the king or immediate ruler, and his laws are taken as the statute-book of the kingdom, these laws being usually administered by a priestly order as his ministers and agents," to something very much less than this.

Augustine does not attempt to define the terms of any union, but it is clear that he intends that the Church should exercise great influence on the Roman State. The chapters at the end of that section of the *City of God* that deals with Rome (V. 24 to end) give a fairly clear impression of what Augustine expects of

Christian emperors of Rome: they should "make their power their trumpeter to divulge the true adoration of God's majesty"; and the repentance of the excommunicated Theodosius is duly approved.

It should be emphasized, just the same, that Augustine did not attempt to determine the sphere of that influence, and the possibility that an emperor, whether Christian or not, might resist such influence could not be discounted at the beginning of the fifth century.

Nevertheless the general position was fairly clear: Rome was fulfilled in Christianity. This idea is set out at length in a letter to Marcellinus, to whom the *City of God* itself is addressed. With an excerpt from it we may conclude:

In the most opulent and illustrious Empire of Rome, God has shown how great is the influence of even civil virtues without true religion, in order that it might be understood that, when this is added to such virtues, men are made citizens of another commonwealth, of which the King is truth, the law is love, and the duration is eternity" [Ep. 138. 17; translation by McCracken in the Loeb series, Vol. I].

Rome's natural virtues are an ideal base on which religion builds the citizen of the city of God.

Epilogue

The approach throughout this book has been to present the *City of God* as a vision of man's destiny springing from Augustine's reflection upon his own life and in particular his conversion.

Augustine's *absolute* position was that only those who gave due worship to the Christian God were truly virtuous and could hope for salvation. Those, therefore, such as the worthies of Rome, who gave worship to many gods, were *absolutely* vicious, and the State they served, in not recognizing the true God, lacked true justice. Similarly Greek philosophy, as represented in Porphyry, who came so very near (as it seemed to Augustine) the Christian truth, was *absolutely* to be rejected because it refused to accept the possibility of an eternal body.

But divine Providence as it had led Augustine

himself through errors and disorders to Christianity, likewise permitted good to arise from what, theologically, must be condemned. One must recall that for Augustine *merely not to serve* God was evil.

Speaking, however, non-theologically, in a *relative* and indeed normal way, Rome, polytheism apart, was not only good but was chosen to prepare, but differently from the Hebrews, for the coming of Christianity in which it was to be fulfilled and prolonged. Platonism, likewise, could be viewed as leading inevitably to Christianity in which its problems, Augustine suggested, were finally resolved. Augustine, of course, was not unaware that neither the polytheistic Roman nor follower of Porphyry would agree with him.

The *City of God* is, therefore, directly more concerned with justifying the Christian prohibition of polytheism than with defending the Christians against the charge of·being responsible for the decline of Rome and its sack in A.D. 410. Its approach is not philosophical in any strict sense; it does not give a theology of history unless by this phrase is meant a view of history in the light of theology. It is not, using the word in its ordinary sense, hostile to the State, which is not founded, in its view, on injustice, as we normally speak of injustice. Neither does the *City of God* rely on a Platonic teaching of an unchangeable law as contrasted with the notion of an unpredictable authority, against which the Reformation is regarded as being a protest.

Although, doubtless under the stress of the Pelagian controversy, the work shows too little optimism in its expectation on the number of men destined for salvation, it reflects the growing confidence of a Church that at once promised to men a beatitude greater than that possible before the Fall and witnessed the thronging of multitudes to submit to its authority. The fulfillment of the prophecies of the Old Testament, the truth contained in the secular oracles and philosophy of Greece and Rome, and the confirmation of Christianity by miracles all strengthened the Christian's faith and hope.

Augustine was not among those who believed that the end of the world was at hand. He left the future to God on whose providence all must depend. In the meantime he would seek to find in all merely human things the good that, as created, they must possess.

If the radical division between the two cities is in the will, if love is the final determinant between their citizens, love is also the dominating quality of Augustine's book. Failure to serve the true God apart, all else he loves; all else he cherishes; all else he freely embraces.

It is this calm confidence for the future and love of the created good that the Christian believer, if he is to follow the lesson of the *City of God*, must now in our time show.

Notes

For a general bibliography, with reference to the *City of God* and giving editions and translations, see that adapted by me in H. I. Marrou, *St. Augustine and His Influence Through the Ages*, New York, Harper Torchbooks; London, Longmans, 1957, pp. 182–190.

For current information on Augustinian studies, see the *Revue des Etudes Augustiniennes* (hereafter referred to as *R.E.A.*), a quarterly with almost complete coverage of books and articles appearing everywhere in connection with Augustinian studies, published at 8 rue François Ier., Paris VIIIe. See also *Augustinus*, which makes a similar attempt, published at Cea Bermúdez, 59, Madrid.

1. Cf. John J. O'Meara, *The Young Augustine* (1954), pp. 115 ff.

2. Cf. *Monumenta Germaniae Historiae, Auctores Antiqui*, ed. O. Seeck (1883), VI. I.

3. Cf. *Ep.* 18.

4. *C. or. Symm.* I. 608.

5. *Ibid.*, I. 587f.

6. *Ciu. Dei* XVIII. 54.

7. *Ep.* 93. 10.

8. A. Lauras and H. Rondet, "Le Thème des deux Cités dans l'œuvre de saint Augustin" (Etudes Augustiniennes, Paris, 1953), pp. 99–160.

9. *Augustinus Magister* (Etudes Augustiniennes, Paris, 1954), III, 202.

10. Cf. C. Lambot, "Lettre inédite de S. Augustin relative au *De civitate Dei*," *Revue Bénédictine*, 51 (1939), pp. 109–121.

11. Cf. VII. 32; X. 8,17; XVII. 16; XVIII. 27ff., 50f.; XXII. 5–8.

12. See John J. O'Meara, *Porphyry's Philosophy from Oracles in Augustine*, (Etudes Augustiniennes, Paris, 1959), p. 63.

13. Cf. *Confessiones* VI. 5f.

14. Cf. H. A. Wolfson, *Philo: Foundations of Religious Philosophy in Judaism, Christianity, and Islam* (Harvard, 1938). See especially I. 103, 142; II. 443.

15. Cf. E. Barker, Introduction to the *City of God* (Everyman's Library, ed. 1947), pp. xvf.

16. For the case against this, see J. Ratzinger, "Beobachtungen zum Kirchenbegriff des Tyconius im 'Liber Regularum,' " R.E.A., II (1956), pp. 173–185.

17. But see H. I. Marrou, *Augustinus Magister* (Paris, 1954), III, 200.

18. Cf. R. T. Marshall, *Studies in the Political and Socio-Religious Terminology of the De Civitate Dei* (Catholic University of America, 1952); G. del Estal and J. R. Rosado, "Equivalencia de 'civitas' en el 'De Civitate Dei,' " *La Ciudad de Dios*, CLXVII (1954), II, pp. 367–454.

19. Cf. J. Ratzinger, *Volk und Haus Gottes in Augustins Lehre von der Kirche* (Munich, 1954).

20. Cf. E. Meuthen, "Der ethische Charakter der civitates bei Augustinus und ihre platonische Fehldeutung," *Aus Mittelalter und Neuzeit* (Bonn, 1957), pp. 43–62; H. I. Marrou, "*Civitas Dei, civitas terrena: num tertium quid?*" *Studia Patristica* (Berlin, 1957), II, pp. 342–350. J.-C. Guy, *Unité et structure logique de la "Cité de Dieu" de saint Augustin* (Paris, 1961), pp. 115 ff.

21. Cf. G. Ladner, *The Idea of Reform: Its Impact on Christian Thought and Action in the Age of the Fathers* (Harvard, 1959), especially pp. 153ff.; for a wider discussion of the *City of God* see *ibid.*, pp. 239ff., and for the history of the principal phases of the idea of such a city in earlier Christian literature see pp. 242ff.

22. See the short bibliography given in H. I. Marrou, *Saint Augustine* . . . mentioned at the head of these notes; e.g., H. Rondet, "Liberté et grâce dans la théologie augustinienne," in *Saint Augustin parmi nous* (Paris, 1954), pp. 201–222, 297–306.

23. Cf. J. Ratzinger, "Herkunst und Sinn der Civitas-Lehre," *Augustinus Magister* (Paris, 1954), II. pp. 965–979, where account is taken of the fundamental work of W. Kamlah, *Christentum und Geschichtlichkeit*, 2nd. ed. (Cologne-Stuttgart, 1951).

24. Cf. V. U. Padovani, *S. Agostino*, supplement to the *Rivista di filosofia neo-scolastica*, t. XXIII (*Milan*, 1931), pp. 220–263; *Filosofia e teologia della storia* (Brescia, 1953), II. pp. 29–75. For a view on its limited possibility, see G. del Estal, *La Ciudad de Dios*, CLXVII, 1954, I. pp. 207–283.

25. For a bibliographical survey and *mise-au-point* see H. I. Marrou, *Augustinus Magister* (Paris, 1954), III. pp. 193ff. and the entries given in his *Saint Augustine* . . .

mentioned at the head of these notes; cf. also J. Chaix-Ruy, S. *Augustin, Temps et Histoire* (Paris, 1956).

26. *Augustinus Magister*, III. pp. 196, 202.

27. J. Perret, *Virgile* (Paris, 1959), p. 115.

28. Cf. John J. O'Meara, *Against the Academics*, Ancient Christian Writers Series, Vol. 12 (1950), pp. 19–22, for a summary description; also "Augustine and Neo-Platonism," in *Recherches Augustiniennes* (Paris, 1958), I. pp. 91–111.

29. "St. Augustine and St. Thomas," in *A Monument to St. Augustine* (London, 1930).

30. Cf. e.g., J. Ratzinger, *Volk u. Haus Gottes* . . . , pp. 262–276, 280; Yves J. M. Congar, " 'Civitas Dei' et 'Ecclesia' chez saint Augustin," in R.E.A., III (1957), pp. 1–14, where there is a select bibliography given.

31. *The Nature and Destiny of Man* (London, 1941); cf. I. p. 171.

32. Cf. "The Two Types of Philosophy of Religion," *Union Seminary Quarterly Review*, I, 1946, No. 4.

33. Cf. "Der Platonismus und die altchristliche Gedankenwelt," *Entretiens sur l'Antiquité classique*, III: *Recherches sur la tradition platonicienne* (Fondation Hardt, Geneva, 1955), pp. 139–179.

34. Cf. *La possibilité d'une philosophie chrétienne* (Louvain, 1956).

35. Cf. *The Young Augustine*, pp. 125f.

36. Cf. *ibid.*, pp. 196f.

37. Cf. Wolfson, *op. cit.*, I. pp. 20, 142.

38. Cf. *Porphyry's Philosophy from Oracles*, pp. 24, 33f., 36f., 51f., 58.

39. Cf. *The Young Augustine*, pp. 134f.

40. *Porphyry's Philosophy from Oracles* (Paris, 1959).

41. Cf. G. Quispel, "Zeit und Geschichte im antiken Christentum," *Eranos-Jahrbuch*, 1951, XXI, pp. 115–140.

42. Cf. E. Hendrikx, "Platonisches und biblisches

Mt. Mercy College Library
Cedar Rapids, Iowa

Denken bei Augustinus," in *Augustinus Magister* (Paris, 1954), I. pp. 285–292.

43. Cf. *The Young Augustine*, pp. 57ff.

44. Galán y Gutiérrez, *Jus Naturae* (Valladolid, 1954), in Chap. IV (pp. 107–160) discusses both the pessimistic views of, e.g., Gierke and von Müller (according to whom Augustine considered the State to be the work of the Devil) and the more optimistic views of, e.g., Reuter, Troeltsch, Baumgartner (according to whom Augustine recognizes the legitimacy of the civil power).

45. J. Feibleman, *Religious Platonism* (London, 1959), p. 172.

46. *The Kingdom of God in America* (Chicago, 1937), p. x.

47. Cf. G. Tavard, "Le thème de la Cité de Dieu dans le protestantisme américain," R.E.A., V (1959), pp. 207–221.

48. Cf. Welldon's edition of the *Ciu. Dei*, pp. 51f.

49. For Stoic ideas in Augustine see G. Verbeke, "Augustin et le stoicisme," *Recherches Augustiniennes*, (Paris, 1958), I, pp. 67ff. For possible traces of skepticism in Augustine see A.-W. Ziegler, *Augustinus Magister* (Paris, 1954), III, pp. 205f.

50. Cf. R. T. Marshall, *op. cit.*, p. 6.

51. Cf. *Porphyry's Philosophy from Oracles*, pp. 16ff.

52. Cf. *Augustinus Magister* (Paris, 1954), III. pp. 205f.

53. Cf. E. von Ivánka, "Römische Ideologie in der 'Civitas Dei,' " *Augustinus Magister* (Paris, 1954), III. 411ff; cf. *ibid.*, pp. 203ff.

54. For further views see H.-X. Arquillière, *L'Augustinisme Politique* (Paris, 1934), especially pp. 45–57; "L'essence de l'Augustinisme politique," *Augustinus Magister* (Paris, 1954), II. pp. 992f.; J. Straub, "Die geschichtliche Stunde des hl. Augustinus, Heilsgeschehen

119

und Weltgeschichte in dem 'Gottesstaat,' " *La Ciudad de Dios*, CLXVII (1954), I. pp. 571–588; F. G. Maier, *Augustin und das Antike Rom* (Stuttgart, 1956); and the discussion in *Augustinus Magister*, III. pp. 204–212.

McAULEY LIBRARY
MT. MERCY COLLEGE
Cedar Rapids, Iowa 52402